Advanced Public Speaking

Advanced Public Speaking

Dynamics and Techniques

Second Edition

Ruth Livingston, PhD

To order additional copies of this book, contact:
Xlibris
1-888-795-4274
www.Xlibris.com
Orders@Xlibris.com
702227

CONTENTS

Chapter Four: Storytelling

Chapter Five: The Motivational Speech

Chapter Six: Interviews

Chapter Seven: Listening for Success

Chapter Eight: The Lecture or Workshop

Chapter Eleven: Special Occasion Speeches

Chapter One

Introduction

The objectives of this chapter are to:

- ✓ Understand the course topics.
- ✓ Comprehend the need for the course.
- ✓ Examine reasons for public speech anxiety.
- ✓ Evaluate ways to harness speech anxiety.
- ✓ Rate speaking ability.
- ✓ Plan to improve

The majority of college curricula require students to take a course that includes instruction in public speaking. Students typically prepare at least one informative and one persuasive-type speech in basic oral intensive classes, as part of the general core course requirements. As a speech professor, the majority of my students enter the first day of their first college speech class with dread. Frequently, students do not understand the need for a speech class on the first day, but later comprehend how learning to develop a speech is beneficial to their everyday conversations as well as to future professional presentations. Basic communication courses teach students to give short speeches to diverse audiences, but there is not enough time for students to consider public address within a variety of professional situations. For example, those entering the workforce need training in presenting impromptu and motivational speeches. Furthermore, people who interact with others in business need to understand how to conduct sales presentations, workshops, meetings, and interviews. The advanced public speaking course builds upon the basics to provide students with instruction and practice so they can adeptly make presentations in a variety of settings.

Topics to Be Covered

This text has eleven chapters. This chapter explains why mastering the art of public speaking is important to almost any professional career. Fear of public speaking can be a hindrance to success. Chapter one explains the phenomena of harnessing your fear so that you can redirect it and use it to your advantage. In the end, there will be discussion questions to start you on the path to becoming an effective speaker in various settings.

Chapter two explains the basic principles of speeches through Aristotle's five canons of rhetoric. The ethos, logos, and pathos from Aristotle's teaching of public speaking will also be explained. Decades of research would suggest that immediacy behaviors in the classroom increases student learning. Immediacy behaviors increase audience understanding, speaker credibility, and speaker likeability. Immediacy behaviors are important in a variety of speaking situations such as lectures, workshops, interviews, sales presentations, motivational speeches, and when conducting a meeting. Chapter three describes what the behaviors are and how they can be developed in a conversation and public address.

Chapter four addresses the art of storytelling. Storytelling has been used as an effective communication tool for as long as humans have been communicating. This chapter will explain how presenters can develop vivid stories to interest and influence an audience. There are exercises to practice the art and to develop a powerful story. Chapter five defines what a motivation speech is and has example topics. One of the organization patterns to be explored is Monroe's Motivated Sequence. A narrative organization pattern will also be explained. The chapter includes motivational techniques such as the use of personal examples, compelling stories, figurative language, emotional appeals, and quotes. A template to prepare a motivational speech is provided.

Interviewing is important throughout one's career. Chapter six gives instruction about how to do well in a job interview, academic interview, and when conducting an interview. Explanations are provided about how to prepare a resume and cover letter. Interviewing tips, which includes researching companies, organizations, job descriptions, and salary scales, are included. A plan to outline key qualities that interviewers will be considering is provided. Additional topics are proper introductions and nonverbal communication that make a good impression. Examples of questions and responses are offered. It is also important that interviewees know what questions to ask at the end of the interview and follow up with a thank you letter. Example questions are also supplied along with a section on how to effectively interview on the phone. Managers who are not successful in interviewing others lose credibility with potential employees and may not recruit the best team members to a company. A section of this chapter is devoted to various interviewing processes. Turning people down, who have been interviewed can be an uncomfortable situation. So techniques to graciously turn people down after an interview are included.

Listening is the most used skill in communication but the least taught. "The most neglected language arts skill at all education levels is listening" (Wolvin & Coakley, 1996, p. 33). Chapter seven explores the importance of learning active listening and provides a curriculum for listening in a variety of communication situations. Students will learn how to effectively take in verbal and nonverbal messages, interpret the messages, and remember information more effectively. Listening is an active process that must be understood and taken seriously in order to improve. A self-assessment is included at the end of the chapter. It would be suggested that readers take the assessment before the lecture and at the end of the course. There is an activity designed to help you improve listening skills.

Chapter eight provides instruction on how to conduct interactive lectures and workshops. A rubric is provided with an evaluation form for a lecture. Students in the course should create a PowerPoint presentation for the lecture. The lectures should include activities to get the audience involved in the topic. Suggestions for involving the audience in discussions, bringing in other media, and the use of visuals are included.

Freshman level college speech courses are designed to teach students to choose topics, write outlines, and present informative and persuasion speeches; however, adults are called upon to present themselves without the luxury of preparation. Chapter nine will assist students in presenting themselves in classroom, social, and business situations where they do not have time to plan ahead. Topics include types of impromptu speeches, how to quickly organize thoughts with an introduction, body, and conclusion, and presentation techniques. In chapter ten you will learn how to sell a product or service to potential customers. This will be a culminating activity in that, a sales presentation incorporates research, powerful listening and delivery techniques, speaking that motivates others to action, and responses to impromptu questioning. The chapter includes a critical thinking group project in which you will create a product, decide who the client(s) will be, and give a sales presentation. The final chapter is special occasion speeches. This chapter explains how to give presentations for different occasions.

Instruction within this text will equip you in preparing for a variety of public speaking situations. The class is designed to include time for each student to give a motivational speech, lecture, impromptu speech, interview, group sales presentation, and special occasion speech. You will also be provided opportunities to improve your listening skills. The course is skills-based, allowing time for students to practice presenting.

Importance of an Advanced Public Speaking Course

The ability to effectively express our ideas is important to obtaining successful careers and relationships. You begin the process of learning to organize and present ideas in your first public speaking class. This course and text is an extension of the basics. Polishing your public speaking abilities will assist you in speaking with authority and confidence. The adept public speaker tends to cause conversational events to be more meaningful and memorable. An exemplary speaker secures the respect of others. The skills that you will build upon in this advanced course is to motivate others, conduct effective meetings, engage in active listening, speak off the cuff, interview, sell yourself, teach others, speak at special occasions, and develop immediacy behaviors.

Harnessing Your Fears

People in various leadership positions will need to speak to groups in a wide range of settings. Are you anxious about giving speeches? So are about 75 percent of all Americans. According to *The Book of Lists*, public speaking is the number one fear in America. McConnell (2009) suggests that those who have not mastered the skills and overcome the fear of public speaking are limiting their promotion opportunities. Professionals need practice and expertise concerning how to speak in various settings in order to enhance career opportunities. Kreiner (2008) posits that public speaking skills in various situations such as meetings, conferences, and ceremonies are essential to business success. Therefore, it is important that you not allow public speaking anxiety to hold you back from reaching your professional potential.

Why We Are Anxious When Presenting

The fear of public speaking is caused by various factors. One reason is that we have feelings of vulnerability. We think we are weak if we are afraid. Yet I do not know of anyone who perceives public speaking as a weakness in others, but individuals perceive any fear that they possess as a personal weakness. It is not a weakness, but a natural response. When you are in front of others speaking, you are looked upon as the expert in the topic, and you may worry that you will do something or say something that will make you appear foolish. If you do, it will soon be forgotten by your audience. Learn to laugh at yourself and move on. Your feelings of vulnerability are internal because you expect more from yourself than your audience expects from you.

To lessen your feelings of vulnerability, realize that your speech will not be perfect. Most of your audience has the fear of public speaking; so they do not view your fear as a weakness. Think of your audience as your friends bunched up on your living room couch, not a sea of eyes scrutinizing your every word. Talk nicely to yourself before you present. Think of the very worst thing that could happen, and how that most hideous and unlikely thing that can happen is not that bad. For example, my greatest fear when speaking is that I will have to go to the restroom when talking. If this happens, I can just excuse myself. The audience will probably find it amusing. I have had students fear that they would throw up during a presentation. Out of the thousands of speeches that I have heard, this has never occurred. I tell my students that if they throw up, I will hold their hair, give them a breath mint, and then we can move on. In the end, the worst that can happen will not. If something unusual or embarrassing does occur, it will give you a great story to discuss with your friends.

Public speaking is a learned skill. If you are not confident in your ability to organize and deliver a speech, you will be nervous. This text and course is designed to equip you with the skills needed to give a great presentation. Although it appears that some people are born with a talent to present, public speaking is a learned skill. The lack of training and experience are good reasons to be nervous. With work, you can learn the art and this course and the activities from the text will provide you with experience. The fear of public speaking almost always reduces with successful experiences.

If you have had a bad past experience, it can cause a fear that the experience will happen again. I have always had a fear of public speaking and have some experiences where my fear caused me to be noticeably nervous. I am the only one who remembers the shaking and quivering. Although I have given hundreds of formal presentations, not including classroom lectures, I still get nervous in front of a new audience. In one recent speech, I did not remove my notes from the lectern after I finished presenting because I was shaking so badly. My boss at the time was in the audience, and for some reason, this made me even more nervous than usual. The speech went well, and now I have another story to tell my students who are nervous about presenting. If you have a past experience where your nervousness was an issue, it is time to laugh (or at least smile) and move on.

A primitive instinct when your body experiences fear is called fight or flight (Dozier, 2007). When you are afraid, your body produces adrenaline that would give you a boost of energy to assist you in fighting a predator or running away. This hormone is what causes you to experience shaking, dry mouth, fidgeting, blushing, heart rate increase, and shortness of breath. You may wonder why I enjoy giving formal presentations if I still get nervous. One of my former students, Adam Hall, said, "I love to present speeches, even though I get scared. It's like bungee jumping without the 'you might die' thing involved." If you are a little anxious or terrified of public speaking, do not let that stop you. Move forward and use the nervousness to your advantage.

Advantages to Nervousness

Use the energy generated by adrenaline to help you. You can funnel this energy to your presentation, making your delivery more exciting. Be energetic. Nervousness is also a good motivator to prepare and practice. You will be less nervous if you know that you are prepared and adept at presenting a speech. Although you never want to be anxiety free (boring), you want to be confident. Be poised in appearance when speaking to your audience. Unless you tell the audience that you are nervous, they will not know. If you announce that you are nervous, you will feel more vulnerable to your audience, and thereby, become more anxious. Act the part, even if you do not feel confident, and be as prepared as possible.

Memorize the first two lines of your presentation, and then use an outline with your main points. *Do not* read a speech! If you are going to read the speech, just give your audience a copy of your essay. Instead, present the speech with energy and goodwill which will be inspirational. In the end, if you learn the skills, practice, and present as if you feel confident, you will give successful presentations. After presenting successfully to the same audience, the nervousness will diminish.

This text is designed to teach you how to give different types of presentations in an array of settings and to improve upon your listening skills. Enhancing your communication skills will be beneficial to you on a personal and professional level. To be willing to present in front of an audience, it is necessary to harness your anxiety about public speaking. Your fear will ease if you do not expect yourself to be perfect, and if you think of your audience as a group of your friends. Talk to them as if you were having a one-on-one conversation. Realize that the worst that could happen is not that bad, and thoroughly prepare for the presentation.

Discussion questions

1. Think about the best presentation that you can remember. Write at least fifteen reasons why this speech and speaker made the presentation meaningful and memorable to you.

    1. _____
    2. _____
    3. _____
    4. _____
    5. _____
    6. _____
    7. _____
    8. _____
    9. _____
    10. _____
    11. _____
    12. _____
    13. _____
    14. _____
    15. _____

    Choose two of the characteristics above that you would like to improve upon and write a paragraph explaining your strategy for improvement.

2. Reflect upon a time that you were nervous about giving a presentation. Tell a person in the class about the event or write about the event.

After explaining this, write down the names of the people in the audience that you think cared about and remembered that you were nervous.

You are probably the only one. If you had a bad experience, it is time to move forward.

3. Although you may become fearful when presenting, you are not going to die. Other than that, write down or tell one other person what you are most fearful about when giving a speech. Then write down or discuss the possibility of your fear coming to pass. Finally, explain how this fear is not that bad in the scope of life and how you plan to move past it.

4. On a scale of one to ten with one being poor and ten being expert, rate yourself as a public speaker.

   What are your goals for improvement? List five goals that you have that you would like to see improved upon when you complete this course.

   a. _____

   b. _____

   c. _____

   d. _____

   e. _____

References

Dozier, R. W. (1999). *Fear itself: The origin and nature of the powerful emotions that shapes our lives and our world.* NY: St. Martin Press.

Kreiner, J. (2008, Aug. 6). *Simple and effective public speaking. Training Time.* Retrieved from http://www.trainingtime.com/npps/story. cfm?nppage=339

Mayo, T. (2009, Feb. 26). *The ultimate motivational speech: 40 inspirational speeches in 2 minutes.* [video recording]. Retrieved November 14, 2009, from http://mayogenuine.com/blog/ the-ultimate-motivational- speech/

McConnell, C. R. (2009, July-Sept). *Effective oral presentations: speaking before groups as part of your job. The Health Care Manager.*, 28, 3. p.264(9). Retrieved from Academic One File via Gale: *http://find. galegroup.com/gtx/infomark.do*? & contentSet=IAC

Monts, B. (2000, Apr.). *Andragogy or pedagogy: A discussion of instructional methodology for adult learners.* Retrieved from http://www.coe.ilstu. edu/scienceed/ci538/papers/monts.htm

Speech Guru. (2005). *Inspirational speech.* Retrieved from http://www. speech-guru.com/inspirational_speech.php

Sullivan, R. & McIntosh, N. (1996). *Delivering effective lectures.* JPIEGO Corp: Baltimore Maryland. Retrieved from http://www. reproline.jhu. edu/english/6read/6training/lecture/delivering_ lecture.htm

Wilson, J. H. & Locker, L., Jr. (2007–2008). *Immediacy scale represents four factors: Nonverbal and verbal components predict student outcomes.* Journal of Classroom Interactions. 42, 2. p. 4–10.

Wolvin, A. & Coakley, C. G. (1996). *Listening*, 5th ed. Boston, MA: McGraw Hill.

Chapter Two

Five Canons of Rhetoric

The objectives of this chapter are to:

- ✓ Explain foundational principles of rhetoric.
- ✓ Describe ethos, logos, pathos.
- ✓ Analyze the five canons of rhetoric.
- ✓ Apply the teachings of Aristotle within a presentation.

The teaching of oral and written communication skills have been a part of schooling curricula for thousands of years. The Greeks and Romans taught rhetorical or persuasive principles that have been built upon and serve as the foundation for the study of public address. Aristotle wrote *The Rhetoric* from 367 to 322 BC; this document is deemed as the most important manuscript concerning persuasion written to date (Golden, Goodwin, Coleman, Golden, & Sproule, 2007). In the second chapter of *The Rhetoric*, Aristotle suggests that three components must be provided by the speaker in order to persuade an audience: ethos, logos, and pathos. Ethos is credibility; logos is logic; pathos is emotion. You may be able to force someone to do something, but this is not the same as persuading someone to change a belief, behavior, or attitude. It is similar to the little boy who was ordered to sit down by his father. The boy plopped down with his arms folded and declared, "I may be sittin' down on the outside, but I'm standin' up on the inside." To change someone's belief, behavior, and attitude is a complex process. In the first portion of the chapter the three components of an effective persuasive presentations, ethos, logos, and pathos, are discussed. Then Aristotle's five canons of rhetoric will be explored.

Ethos

The first component that must be present to persuade, motivate, or sell another person is ethos or speaker credibility. For a speaker to obtain credibility, the audience must believe that the speaker is competent, of good character, has the best interests of the audience at heart, and is likeable. Consider a time that you have been persuaded to change a belief, behavior, or attitude by another individual. For instance, think of the last person who sold you a car. At the time, you believed that the salesperson was knowledgeable about the cars you looked at. You probably thought that this salesperson had your best interests at heart and was not trying to scam you. One often goes to a car lot leery of car salespeople, and the car salesperson knows this. Therefore, he or she will say things to make you feel more at ease. In the process, you will grow to trust and like the person who eventually sells you a vehicle. Purchasing a vehicle is one of the most expensive buys most people make, next to a house. Successful salespeople are able to convince others that they are credible by being confident, yet friendly. They radiate immediacy behaviors that enhance likeability.

Competence is displayed when a speaker talks about a topic with confidence. Delivering information that is understandable and well-structured assists the speaker in the appearance of competence. Research your topic or product to such a degree that you can share information without reading. It is okay to have notes, but reading a speech makes you appear incompetent. It is also important that the information is well structured so your audience can understand what you are talking about. Every presentation should include an introduction, body, and conclusion, even a one-minute sales pitch. Use words that your audience understands. We do not like to consider that the reason I do not understand what you are talking about is a limitation on my ability to learn. We would rather think that we do not understand because of the presenter's inability to explain the information. Therefore, consider your audience and speak on their level, without being condescending.

Initial credibility is when the audience believes that the speaker is credible to discuss the topic before the presentation begins. It is proper protocol to introduce a keynote speaker to establish initial credibility. A speech of introduction is a one—to two-minute presentation that explains why the speaker is an expert on the topic to be discussed. Boring introduction speeches go through a full list of credentials. Instead, highlight the speaker by describing the expertise and credentials the speaker has in the subject area. If an introduction speech goes on too long, it depletes the audience's attention rather than provide initial credibility to the speaker. Keynote speakers should not have to explain why they are the experts in their field or this will take away from likeability. A speaker who begins a speech by telling the audience that he or she is a renowned expert will turn an audience away. The audience needs to perceive the speaker as credible, not arrogant. If you are going to be a keynote speaker at an event, send a brief introduction that you will request be read before you present.

If a speaker does not have someone to tell about her credentials on the topic before presenting, then she will need to let the audience know without appearing conceited. One way to do this is to tell a personable story about how this topic affected your life. This should be the attention grabber or be in the introduction of the presentation. For example, if you wanted to sell a fishing pole, tell a story about how you reeled in a prize fish using this rod. A speaker who gave a persuasive speech about texting and driving, told a story about when he had been seriously injured when a texting driver hit him, while he was walking through a parking lot.

If you do not have a personable story about the topic, explain to the audience why you are enthusiastic about the topic and that you have done extensive research. You can mention that you have had an interest in the topic for a specific number of years and what you discovered in your research. For example, if I wanted to persuade my audience that I am competent to talk about the use of immediacy behaviors, I could say, "About eight years ago, I read a book by Virginia Richmond and James McCroskey called *Power in the Classroom*. Through that book and in additional research over the past eight years, I discovered how immediacy behaviors are invaluable to communication within public address and interpersonal relationships." Explain early why you are competent to discuss your topic and why the topic is important to you.

Derived credibility is obtained while you are presenting. This can be gained by presenting powerfully, using effective delivery techniques. The best delivery techniques are those that enhance likeability or use immediacy behaviors, which are explained in chapter three. The speaker must have initial credibility and then maintain a high level of trust throughout the presentation. Lucas (2009) defines derived credibility as, "the credibility of the speaker produced by everything she or he says and does during the speech itself" (p. 353). A speaker that the audience initially believes is credible may lose credibility, if he or she appears incompetent or uncaring.

Terminal credibility is the influence the speaker has on the audience after the speech has concluded (Beebe & Beebe, 2009). It is essential that you have a well-planned, powerful conclusion that leaves a positive and lasting impression. An abrupt or weak conclusion will damage terminal credibility. I was excited to listen to a speaker who was a well-known author. The initial credibility of the speaker was high as audience members anticipated the presentation, holding books for a signing afterward. The presentation was not well organized. He told stories about his life, but the speech lacked new information. All of the stories were also in his book. He jumped incoherently from one topic to another, and then he ended abruptly. Terminal credibility was low, and the crowd of those wanting their books signed dwindled. Enhance terminal credibility by being well prepared and ending with powerful final words. Ethos or credibility must be maintained from the introduction to the conclusion of your presentation. This is accomplished by being confident, knowledgeable, and likeable throughout.

Logos

Logos or a logical appeal is important when persuading an audience, especially one that disagrees with you. When using a logical appeal, show credible evidence to support your claim. A believable logical appeal will clearly state your case and then back up your claim with appropriate reasoning. "Reasoning is the process of drawing a conclusion from evidence" (Beebe & Beebe, 2009, p. 382). A logical claim that is backed by evidence should lead to a natural conclusion. For example, you may claim that fatty foods that are conveniently accessed at fast-food restaurants are causing a higher number of children to become obese. The argument is backed by research that children who are eating at fast-food restaurants are more prone to obesity (Holguin, 2003). A clear look at the research provides a convincing argument of the claim. "The new study results bolster evidence that fast food contributes to increased calorie intake and obesity risk in children," Yale University obesity researcher Kelly Brownell said in an accompanying editorial (Holguin, 2003, par. 12). The claim is convincingly plausible. The fact that one-third of children in the United States get at least one meal at a fast-food restaurant every day leads to the conclusion that such eating habits contribute to the increase of child obesity (Holguin, 2003). You show the evidence for an unprecedented number of children eating at fast-food restaurants, fast-food restaurants having a menu of fatty foods, and the rate of childhood obesity on the rise. This evidence then leads to the conclusion that children who regularly eat at such establishments are more prone to obesity.

The above example implements inductive reasoning. "Using this classical approach, you reach a general conclusion based on specific examples, facts, statistics, and opinions" (Beebe & Beebe, 2009, p. 383). The evidence links fast-food restaurants with increasing childhood obesity in the United States.

The opposite approach is deductive reasoning. This is when you state a general principle that children who eat regularly at fast-food restaurants are more prone to childhood obesity, and then reach a conclusion that parents should not take their children to fast-food restaurants. Such a claim can be termed as a syllogism. For example, my nephew eats at a fast-food restaurant every day. My nephew is morbidly obese. Therefore, children who regularly eat at fast-food establishments are more prone to obesity. Deductive reasoning suggests that your reasoning is certain (Beebe, Beebe & Ivy, 2007).

Cause and effect is another logical approach. This is when you link an outcome to a cause. For example, people who have college degrees make more money than those who do not have a degree. Therefore, the cause of obtaining a college degree can be linked to the effect of making more money. This is a causal relationship that is plausible. Causal fallacies occur when there is a relationship but there is not a plausible link. This is called post hoc fallacy.

For example, when ice cream sales increase in America, the crime rate goes up (Salkind, 2007). Does eating ice cream cause crime? Of course not. This is an exaggerated example of post hoc or causal fallacy.

However, there are many links that people have made using statistics that are also post hoc fallacies. It is best to bring in additional evidence that helps make your claim rather than isolated causal relationships. Does texting while driving cause accidents? People who text while driving are more likely to be in an accident. Distracted driving has been linked to 80 percent of vehicle accidents, so it would be logical to suggest that text messaging while driving contributes to automobile accidents (Vogel, 2007).

There are other fallacies that should be avoided. Below are common fallacies (Beebe, Beebe & Ivy, 2007; Lucas, 2009; O'Hair, Rubenstein, & Stewart, 2007).

Bandwagon fallacy makes the claim that because a belief is popular, you should believe it too. Or that if a product is popular or being used by people who are popular, then you should purchase the product as well. Think of times in history that the majority were doing the wrong thing. Just because a majority of people in a given area are opposed to equal rights for gays and lesbians does not mean that a group of citizens should be marginalized. Such a claim would be a bandwagon fallacy.

Red herring is an attempt to divert the audience from an issue by bringing up an irrelevant issue. It is suggested that fox hunters used to rub a fish on the ground to divert their hunting dogs from a trail. The red herring fallacy was used by Richard Nixon in his speech, "Checkers." In 1952, Nixon was accused of the unethical use of money in a political fund and the accepting of gifts. He deflected the issue of mishandling money by bringing up a gift that was not even in question. After the speech, there was an outpour of support for him to stay on the Eisenhower ticket as vice president.

Red herring fallacy usually uses some type of emotional appeal that moves people away from the topic at hand, as Nixon did by bringing up a puppy for his six-year-old daughter.

Another way to divert an audience away from the real issue is *ad hominem*. *Ad hominem* is when one person attacks another person even though the attack has nothing to do with the issue. This is frequently done in politics and masses have been led astray by such attacks. The fallacy is most effective with an audience who has prejudices or special interests. For instance, "What does he know about balancing the budget? He's a liberal." or, "How can you believe a thing that she says? She is an atheist." Such attacks do not relate to the issues but divert people by bringing up biases. This is an unethical distortion.

Either-or fallacy gives the option of two choices when more exist. This has also been called the black or white policy. There are a vast number of opportunities and decisions that fall into the gray. Few problems that we solve are as simple as either-or decisions. Either-or fallacy is a polarized view of the world. It is the "If you ain't fer me yer again me," mentality. Examples include, "Either you wear a seat belt or you will die." Although one should wear a seat belt, this type of reasoning is a fallacy and too simplistic. Make the case more convincingly. You can discuss the staggering statistics of those who have been saved by wearing seat belts when in automobile accidents, and then bring up the counter arguments of the fewer number who survived accidents when thrown from the vehicle. The point is that wearing a seat belt increases your chances of survival but does not promise survival. In the end, provide your audience with accurate information.

Slippery slope is an exaggerated claim that once you do one thing, this will lead to the demise of humankind. It is an assumption that one small step will lead to unpreventable ensuing steps. I read an article that suggested that if marijuana was legalized in the United States, it would lead to an epidemic of poverty, alcohol abuse, death, overdose, and crime. "It seems as those drugs eventually leads to all of these circumstances" (123HelpMe.com). I do not know the result of legalization of marijuana in America, but that the legalization will lead to our nation falling into poverty, alcoholism, and crime is a slippery slope fallacy. Not all slippery slopes are fallacies. A quote by William Henry III about falsehoods may be a true slippery slope. "Any departure from fact is the first step on a slippery slope toward unbelievability." The slippery slope fallacy is best avoided by not making outlandish claims that one step will cause exaggerated consequences. Instead of making false assumptions, provide evidence that decisions in the past has led to undesirable circumstances.

Transference occurs when we redirect our feeling about one thing onto something else. Sigmund Freud suggested that we often transfer our feelings about one person onto another person (Dombeck, 2005). If you meet someone for the first time and immediately dislike the person, you may be transferring your feelings on that person from the feelings that you have for another person who harmed you in the past. There may be a look or mannerism that the person from your past and this stranger share. The same can be true of transferring an idea onto another idea that is not similar. For instance, I read an article where a group was claiming that condoms being offered to high school students at school was the cause for promiscuous sex among teens. They were transferring an unwanted behavior, promiscuous sex, by giving away condoms. It has been a while since I was in high school, but I do not see the connection. I cannot imagine a seventeen-year-old boy walking down the halls of his high school, peering into the nurse's station, and seeing a sign for a free condom, and that being the first time he thinks about having sex. The free condom was not the cause. One should be careful to not transfer one idea on something that is not related. Pragmatically consider your opinions and positions based upon fact.

More than 125 fallacies have been identified (Lucas, 2009). The main thing to remember when developing a logical argument is to gather facts and evidence. This should lead to a plausible conclusion. Avoid fallacies and watch for misleading concepts in speeches and in writings. Those who are emotional about particular issues tend to be more vulnerable to fallacies. It is okay to bring out the points of an argument that do not line up with your beliefs. You can be open-minded and not be wishy-washy. A healthy, intellectual discussion views the points and the evidence open-mindedly and logically.

Pathos

Pathos is the term Aristotle used to describe the stirring of emotions (Honeycutt, 2004). Although an argument should be constructed with logical evidence, people will be moved to action when their emotions are stirred. It has been argued that this is unethical; however, emotional appeals that are honest and sincere are certainly ethical. Listen to the emotional appeals of speakers like Martin Luther King Jr. or Edward Kennedy's eulogy for Robert Kennedy. These are powerful speeches that stirred emotions within audience members.

When writing a speech, imagine the emotions that you want your audience to experience. Aristotle provides numerous examples of emotions that stir audiences to action: anger and calmness, friendship and enmity, fear and confidence, shame and shamelessness, kindness and unkindness, pity, indignation, envy, and emulation or ambition. He also suggested additional motivators such as wealth and power (Honeycutt, 2004). It is wise that people are not stirred to have negative emotions aimed toward the speaker, but are moved to consider issues that cause them harm. For example, it would be a positive approach to explain how a college degree assists individuals in acquiring careers that help them provide a better life for their families (emulation). A negative approach to the same topic would be to scold the audience for failure. Fear appeals is another negative emotion.

Fear is sometimes used unethically, and it often does not have a lasting effect. For an audience to be moved by fear, they must feel vulnerable, and be provided a way to relieve the fear. After 9/11, we, as a nation, felt vulnerable by the thought that terrorists could murder so many people, and we did not have control over this. The government had terror alerts of different colors like red, orange, blue, and yellow, but was slow to tell us what to do in case of an attack. Americans had no idea about what to do if we went to a high terror alert. Finally, the American public was given instructions about how to prepare for a terrorist attack. The instruction given was to buy disaster supplies such as duct tape, plastic sheeting, and bottled water. Stores sold out, and then people began to wonder how these supplies would protect them from attacks such as the ones on 9/11 (Dunn, 2003). Because we were not offered solutions, we stopped worrying about the color codes of terror and moved on with our lives. If you cannot provide your audience with a reasonable way to relieve the fear that you evoke, then you should use a more positive emotion than fear when developing a persuasive speech.

Consider stirring positive emotions in people such as showing them how their ambition can help them succeed. If you show an audience that they have lost power over their own behaviors, it will cause them to want to change. I quit smoking for ten years. I had heard the fear and shame appeals, but simply justified my actions. Then I got pneumonia. Rather than quitting smoking, I smoked menthol cigarettes so it would not burn my lungs. Then I realized that I did not have power and control over my own life. I was allowing cigarettes to control my life. I started thinking about how the cravings were controlling my behaviors. With that in mind, I made it my New Year's resolution and quit smoking.

This is also an example of cognitive dissonance. If you can convince someone her or his beliefs do not match up with his or her behaviors, the person will either change his belief, or change her behavior, or he or she will be most uncomfortable. We do not want to remain in dissonance. When I made the decision to quit smoking, I needed to believe that I was in control of my own life. When I discovered that cigarettes controlled my behavior to such an extent that I continued to smoke while having pneumonia, I decided to quit smoking. Emotions are closely tied to the needs that we have for self-efficacy. Showing an audience that their beliefs and values are linked to your ideologies or topic will be the turning point to changing behavior or attitudes.

Aristotle suggested using pathos within the conclusion. Emotions can be stirred throughout as long as you have backed your claims with evidence. But bring in an emotional close. You consider the emotional tone that you would like to create and construct your speech accordingly. When giving a persuasion speech, give a passionate challenge that yields results.

Five Canons of Rhetoric

Aristotle and other Greek scholars suggested that rhetoric or public discourse had five established principles: invention, arrangement, style, memory, and delivery. These canons have been taught as a foundation for public address for thousands of years, and are still believed to be the foundation of rhetorical theory and education. The principles have the basics of preparing and delivering presentations (Burton, 2001).

Invention

Invention is the first rhetorical process defined by Aristotle (Lauer, 2004). It is why the speech is created and how to construct the speech for the desired effect. Any invention that has been made, started with a need, a reason. Inventors use innovation to solve a problem. Look around you. Everything from the bookshelf to your chair to your curtain was invented by someone to solve a particular problem. When you invent a presentation, consider the need at hand. From there you will consider the needs of your audience, the purpose of presenting, the best way to present, the emotions you will stir within the audience, and the time frames that you have been given. After you have considered these things, you will come up with the topic or the name of your invention.

When creating your speech, you may discover new knowledge or build upon the insights of others. Either way, you are to innovatively construct knowledge that you will present to others. No matter how much knowledge and experience that you have on a chosen topic, seek out new information. The invention process of research and development should be a journey or search for wisdom. Although you may have a wealth of knowledge on a given subject, there are always new gems to be discovered. Scholars have suggested that not only is knowledge presented in a more effective manner through rhetoric, but rhetoric also constructs knowledge (Lauer, 2004). Invention brings about a study of discovery or a heuristic process.

> Heuristic procedures are thought to engage memory and imagination and are able to be taught and transferred from one situation to another. While students typically use heuristics deliberately while learning them, more experienced creators often use them tacitly, shaping them to their own styles. (Lauer, 2004, p. 9)

Consider the possibilities as you consider the need, and invent a presentation that will meet the needs of your audience, and those that your audience will influence.

Arrangement

How the speech is arranged depends upon the type of speech, although all speeches should have an introduction, body, and conclusion. In the introduction, you gain the audience's attention using an attention grabber: tell a dramatic story, arouse curiosity, startle your audience, explain how the topic relates to their lives, ask a question, use a startling statistic, refer to a current event, or use humor. These techniques are explained in detail in the motivational speech chapter. After you have gained the attention of the audience, establish your credibility by describing your expertise in that you have an experience with the topic or that you have researched the topic. It is important to establish identification or make a connection with those listening at the beginning of your speech. Then tell them what you are going to tell them in the form of a preview.

Within the body of your speech, you will establish a need, introduce a problem, and explain the facts. Back up your claims with supported evidence, illustrations, anecdotes, statistics, research data, and examples. Make your stories as vivid as possible. At the end of your presentation, you will signal your conclusion with a statement such as, "in conclusion." Then summarize what you have said. Do not add any new information. Your final words should be memorable. Aristotle suggested stirring emotions or the use of pathos to close the speech. A call to action or a final challenge comprise the best endings for a persuasive speech. You can also end with a quote or tie back to the attention grabber, but give the audience a challenge or something to do with the information you have presented. However you end, make it as powerful as possible. Leave them wanting more.

There are four common organizational styles for persuasive speeches. Problem solution establishes that there is a problem. First, state the problem and then give evidence that the problem exists and has an effect on the audience members. Then provide a solution. I have watched documentaries and read articles that established that a societal problem existed, but did not offer a way that I could help resolve the problem. This is unfair and pointless. When you work on a problem in any relationship, work on the problem and have possible solutions to consider with the person you are in conflict with. Do not even discuss issues that are unsolvable. Similarly, if your audience cannot assist in solving a problem that you want to address, choose another topic. The solution you suggest should be doable for the audience members and something that you are doing. Problem, cause, solution is similar to problem/solution except you show the cause. The causes will more than likely lead to a natural solution to the problem.

Monroe's Motivated Sequence is an organizational style that was published by Alan Monroe in 1939. This arrangement is fully explained in the motivational chapter of the text. The five sections of Monroe's Motivated Sequence are attention, need, satisfaction, visualization, and action. It is an effective organizational pattern for developing a motivational speech. Persuasion speeches can also be arranged with advantages and disadvantages. This is where you bring up the pros and cons, and then explain why your claim has the most advantages.

Careful arrangement of a speech will enhance audience understanding and will assist the audience in recalling your speech later. Every presentation, from the one-minute impromptu speech to the three-hour lecture, should have a distinct introduction, body, and conclusion. Within the body, you should have a clear organizational pattern. Also, between each section of your speech and between each point, make clear transitions. A well-structured speech assists your audience in following you through the scenic route of valuable information, and then remembering what you discussed.

Style

The ideology of style adds the aesthetic ornamentation to a presentation. Aristotle wrote, "For it is not enough to know *what* we ought to say; we must also say it as we ought; much help is thus afforded towards producing the right impression of a speech" (Honeycutt, Book III, Chapter 1). It is the choice of words. Within style, one must rid a presentation of grammatical errors, offensive language, and fill the speech with powerful imagery and figurative language such as metaphors, similes, antithesis, repetition, and parallelism.

A speaker who butchers the English language will not gain credibility from an audience. A common grammatical error deals with irregular verbs. If you have difficulty using irregular verbs correctly, get an English book and learn the proper usage. Ask those who listen to you speak, to point out grammatical errors so you can work to improve your speech. Discover one or two incorrect grammar habits that you can eliminate from your everyday conversations. Sometimes you know a phrase is incorrect, but you say it out of habit. Below is a list of twenty common errors and the correct usage.

Incorrect	Correct
I think I did good on the test.	I think I did well on the test.
Me and my brother went home.	My brother and I went home.
She don't want to continue working here.	She doesn't want to continue working here.
You should have went to the party.	You should have gone to the party.
Irregardless of what you think, I like her.	Regardless of what you think, I like her.
James should have gave me a turn.	James should have given me a turn.
You wanna wash the car?	Would you like to wash the car?
Would you like to go with my cousin and myself to the beach?	Would you like to go to the beach with my cousin and me?
I had wrote the essay.	I wrote the essay.
I can run more faster, now.	I can run faster now.
I don't got no work boots.	I don't have work boots.
She went and got her hair cut.	She got a haircut.
I drug my best friend to the mall.	I dragged my best friend to the mall.
I have came to help you.	I have come to help you.
I had ran out of gas on my way to work.	I ran out of gas on my way to work.
Jerry seen the whole thing.	Jerry saw the whole thing.
I am real worried about Ann.	I am really worried about Ann.
I have rode on a Ferris wheel.	I have ridden on a Ferris wheel.
We have spoke about this before.	We have spoken about this before.
The paper said that it would snow.	The meteorologist said that it would snow.

When you are presenting, it is important that you use language that is not offensive. Although the subject of political correctness has been the brunt of jokes, use unbiased language in speeches. Choose language that promotes equality and dignity for all people. Avoid language that is sexist, heterosexist, ageist, racist, or insensitive in any way. Gays and lesbians prefer gay and lesbian, and any other language is unacceptable. Use deaf and hard of hearing rather than hearing impaired. It is incomprehensible that an individual would pick a particular race, gender, religion, political affiliation, or sexual orientation and malign the group by using offensive language. If I hear this kind of language, I let the person know that I am offended. Do not allow anyone to put their hateful trash in your ears.

Although profanity is not offensive to everyone, it should not be used in formal speeches or presentations. I heard a wonderful speaker who used two "curse" words in her thirty-minute presentation. I was not offended, but I spoke with three audience members after the speech who spoke only about being offended by the speaker's profanity. The people who were offended by the two words of profanity only recalled those two words of the speech. It is best to not use language that would offend others if it can be avoided.

When describing a scene or telling a story, you should paint a detailed picture using your words. Think about what you want your audience to see, hear, taste, smell, and feel. Use descriptive words to allow them to explore their senses. Also, use verbs that are descriptive and unique. The excerpt is from Oprah Winfrey's acceptance speech when she received the first Bob Hope Humanitarian Award on September 22, 2002. It vividly describes a story that explains her point and assists her and her audience in making a connection.

Vivid stories, like this one, draw us in. They give us a glimpse of a life, an idea, a belief that could not be experienced any other way. Another way to increase comprehension within a speech is by using figurative language.

Metaphors compare two things that would not normally be compared. The metaphor draws images in the listener's mind that provides a richer understanding. Martin Luther King Jr. used metaphors throughout his speeches, and this tool gave us new perspectives. One of the many examples of metaphor in King's famous "I Have a Dream" speech, "Now is the time to lift our nation from the quick sands of racial injustice to the solid rock of brotherhood." Racial injustice is compared to quicksand, and brotherhood is compared to a solid rock.

Aristotle suggested that a metaphor did not merely add an artistic imagery in the speech, but promoted cognition or learning. Professor Christof Rapp (2002) explains Aristotle's posit that metaphors promote cognition:

> In order to understand a metaphor, the hearer has to find something common between the metaphor and the thing which the metaphor is referred to. For example, if someone calls the old age "stubble," we have to find a common genus to which old age and stubble belong; we do not grasp the very sense of the metaphor until we find that both, old age and stubble, have lost their bloom. Thus, a metaphor does not only refer to a thing, but simultaneously describes the respective thing in a certain respect. This is why Aristotle says that the metaphor brings about learning: as soon as we understand why someone uses the metaphor "stubble" to refer to old age, we have learned at least one characteristic of old age. (Rapp, 2002, 8.2, par. 7)

The use of metaphor bestows a learning experience as the listener is provided with a dynamic view of the issue.

Similes are similar to metaphors in that they make comparisons, but do so using "like" or "as." A simile explaining my love for coffee could be: My first sip of coffee in the morning is like drinking in a ray of morning sun. Be creative when coming up with metaphors and similes. Avoid overused phrases called clichés. Common clichés that are also similes include dry as a bone, fit as a fiddle, and cute as a button.

Antithesis contrasts two ideas. A famous antithesis was from John F. Kennedy's (1961) inaugural address: "Ask not what your country can do for you—ask what you can do for your country." Another example is from Lynden B. Johnson's (1965) "We Shall Overcome" speech: "Equality depends, not on the force of arms or tear gas, but depends upon the force of moral right—not on recourse to violence, but on respect for law and order." The contrasting concepts provide the speaker with sharp distinctions that are memorable.

Repetition is important to retention. You tell the audience your main points in the preview of your presentation, elaborate on these points in the body, and summarize your position in the conclusion. Repetition of phrases may also be used to etch an idea in the memory of individuals.

The repetition of "I Have a Dream" presented by Martin Luther King Jr. has been repeated because it sparks hope in those who have a dream for equality. Consider the most important point that you want your audience to remember. Repeat this idea throughout your presentation.

Parallelism is similar to repetition in that it arranges similar phrases to provide a rhythmic effect. Margaret Chase Smith used parallelism in her speech delivered on June 1, 1950, titled "Declaration of Conscience." "I speak as a Republican. I speak as a woman. I speak as a United States Senator. I speak as an American." Then she went on to elaborate on each of these titles.

When creating your presentations, consciously consider the style of your speech. Style is not using flattery. It is crafting words that will leave a lasting impression on the listeners. Think about the most important idea that you would like your audience to remember. Provide powerful imagery that will help your audience comprehend the benefit of your topic. Fashion your words using unique verbs, metaphors, similes, antitheses, repetitions, and parallelisms. Be careful to use correct grammar. Do not use words that could be offensive. This will put up barriers. Draw your images and provide a friendly environment that will encourage everyone listening while providing a positive, memorable experience.

Memory

During Aristotle's day, orators memorized their speeches. This is the greatest change in speech giving today. Before the printing press, people relied more on memory (McCarthy, 2007). The Ancient Greeks taught oratory students to memorize their speeches in three sections. Speakers were to recite each section facing a different part of the room. Speech forensics students use a similar movement style when presenting. The general rule is to use movement for effect. "Most Declamation pieces I have seen have the speaker start center, go left/right, move left/right, back center, and then down towards the audience for the conclusion" (Forensics Community, 2009, par. 9). Although you will memorize the first few lines of your speech and know your points, do not try to memorize the speech in its entirety. Memorized speeches do not allow for adapting to the audience and often sound canned. Never read your presentation.

Speeches from public officials that need to be read are put on teleprompters. Unless the speech must be read for reasons of national security or absolute accuracy, it is best that the speech be delivered extemporaneously. Do not write your speech word-for-word and bring that to the lectern or else you will read it. Write an extensive outline and use this when you begin practicing your presentation. Then type your main points on one or two pieces of paper. Use spaces between points and use a 14-to 16-point font that is easy to read. Place the paper(s) on the lectern and do not have anything such as note cards or a pen in your hands. I have seen speakers who continually play with objects they are holding such as note cards, pens, or paper clips, and this is a distraction.

There is an element of memorization that will occur when preparing an extemporaneous presentation. I would suggest that you memorize the first two lines of the speech. One of the greatest fears when speaking is that the person's mind will go blank when beginning the speech. Memorize the first few lines to help you get started. You may also want to type the first two lines on your presentation notes to give you confidence that you will not forget how to get started. You may also want to memorize the quotes you will use so you can say them more dramatically; however, quotes can be read. Keep your quotes short, one or two lines. Long quotes or reading poems is boring. You may want to memorize your last two lines so that you know that your speech will end as powerfully as possible. When I practice a speech, I do have parts of it memorized because I have practiced so many times. Nevertheless, the speech that I present is always different than the one that I practice. I add ideas and forget points. When my audience is responding well to an idea, I may elaborate more on that point. My speech is not going to include everything I know on the subject, so I may want to provide more information than previously planned. I may also see quizzical expressions and repeat or rephrase a point to clarify. A completely memorized speech does not allow for such adaptations and spontaneity.

Although the teaching of memory as it relates to oratory education has changed since the time of Aristotle, it does have a place in public address. The speaker should prepare an extensive outline, practice using that outline, and then create condensed notes to take to the lectern. For a five-minute speech, the preparation outline may be two to three pages long with 12-point font. The notes that are used at the lectern during the presentation will be condensed to one page, using 14- to 16-point font. You may want to type the first two sentences and the last two sentences on your lectern notes to help you feel more confident.

Delivery

Before Aristotle, little consideration was given to speech delivery (Fortenbaugh, 2003). When delivery was taught by the Ancient Greeks, emphasis was placed on tone of voice and gestures. Gideon Burton (2001) of Brigham Young University suggests that effective delivery is important to Aristotle's principles of logos, ethos, and pathos. "Delivery obviously has much to do with how one establishes ethos and appeals through pathos, and in this sense is complementary to Invention, which is more strictly concerned with logos" (Burton, 2001, par. 4). In other words, effective delivery is essential to maintain your credibility, bring your audience through your logical claims, and stir emotions that will move them to action. Delivery techniques will be explained in depth in the Immediacy Behavior chapter as this section provides only a brief consideration of gestures and voice.

Every person is unique. Your delivery should line up with your personality. Use gestures that are natural for you. I am an animated person and use many gestures when speaking face-to-face and in front of an audience. It is difficult for me to stand behind a lectern. If you do not gesture naturally, then place your hands on the lectern. Do not grip the lectern or lean, but placing your hands down in front of you is fine if you are not an animated person.

Although a formal speech should have polished language, the delivery style should be conversational. If you are not comfortable with gesturing, plan a few simple gestures to help make a point. For instance, if you are saying that it took you four days to get to San Francisco, hold up four fingers. If you tell about a time when you closed your eyes and jumped off the diving board, you may want to act this out. Only add a few gestures for practice in your next speech if gesturing makes you uncomfortable. You may want to move to various points in the room to help you get away from the lectern. Do not pace. Have a purpose for your movements. Watch fidgeting with your fingers and hair or shifting from one foot to another. Look poised, no matter how you feel, and avoid distracting movements. The best speakers make you feel like they are having a face-to-face conversation with you. It appears natural.

You should make good eye contact by looking at one person in the room, completing a thought, and moving to another person. Look at audience members in the eye and move your eyes in a natural way around the room. If you are speaking to a large crowd, look around the room as naturally as possible. When a speaker is up on a podium speaking to a large audience with blinding lights, it is best to look at the audience, imagining that you are talking to them in the same way. Make it appear that you are talking and connecting to individuals in the audience, even if you cannot see them.

Your rate, pitch, and volume of your speech set the tone or mood of the presentation. If you are discussing something sad, you will want to lower your pitch, slow your rate, and speak in a somber tone. If you want your audience to be happy and energetic, you need to have a higher pitch, speak faster, and raise the volume of your voice to demonstrate that emotion. Vary your volume and pitch throughout the speech. Speak slowly enough that you enunciate clearly, but not so slowly that you sound condescending. Again, this should be a natural, conversational style that is comfortable to you and your audience.

Beware of vocalized pauses such as "um," "and um," "like," etc. If you use vocalized pauses in your everyday conversation, work to omit them. These fillers weaken your communication. Instead, use silent pauses. Use a silent pause after you ask a question, when you have made a point that you want to sink in, or when you have momentarily lost your train of thought. If you forget your next point, take a breath, look down at your notes, and act as though you are reflecting. You will remember if you give yourself a moment. Do not criticize yourself or say something like, "I can't remember what I was going to say." Simply move on to something that you do remember and go back to it. People who play musical instruments are told to continue playing as if nothing happened if they make a mistake. It is the same with public speaking. If you mess up, do not announce it; keep going.

Aristotle was possibly the first rhetorician who emphasized delivery. Effective delivery techniques provide the orator credibility and can stir emotion. Use natural gestures and eye contact. Rather than using a monotone voice, set the mood of your presentation with vocal variety. Omit vocalized pauses such as "um" and replace them with silent pauses to add effect. Appear as poised as possible, never self-criticizing.

Summary

The basis for public address curricula today has drawn from the teachings of Aristotle. He established three components essential to public address which is ethos or credibility, logos or logic, and pathos or emotion. He also established that rhetoric or public discourse had five established principles: invention, arrangement, style, memory, and delivery. Invention is constructing the right words to meet a need. Arrangement is the order in which the speech is created. The speech needs to be organized to be effective. Style provides the speech an aesthetic appeal but is important to providing the audience an understandable, yet memorable experience. Although the adept orator today does not memorize a speech word for word as the Ancient Greeks were taught to do, the main points should be memorized. The speech should also be practiced many times in preparation. Delivery deals with gestures, vocal variety, movement, eye contact, and silent pauses. A speech that meets a need, is understood, is memorable, and well delivered incorporates the five canons of rhetoric.

Five Canons of Rhetoric Assignment

While listening to *The Last Lecture*, explain how Randy Pausch used the five canons of rhetoric by answering the questions below.

Invention
Why did he invent this speech? What are the needs he wanted to meet?

Analyze the audience
People

Environment

Internal and external noise

Did he develop logical arguments? Explain.

Arrangement

Did his introduction gain audience attention? Explain.

Orient the audience? Explain.

Lead to the body? Explain.

What were his propositions or main points?

Identify some of the connectives or transition between points.

Did his conclusion provide a memorable wrap-up? Explain.

Style

Identify powerful words or phrases that made the speech more effective.

Identify three uses of repetition, metaphors, and/or similes.

Memory

Because this presentation is more than an hour long, it would have been difficult to memorize. What portions of the speech do you think he did memorize?

Delivery

Describe how his delivery technique provided him with credibility and emotional appeals.

Did he connect with the audience? How?

Comment on his use of vocal variety and gestures.

Write about the time he took to deliver the speech. Should it have been longer, shorter? Explain.

Write a one paragraph summary of your overall feelings about this presentation.

Working on Style

1. Consider two words or phrases that you would like to remove from your everyday conversations that may slip into your speeches. This could include a grammar error, vocalized pause, or a mispronounced word. One phrase that I am working to remove from my conversations is "a lot." I heard someone say that "a lot is a plot of land." I would like to be more descriptive rather than using this overused phrase. If you cannot think of two things to work on, ask someone that you communicate with on a regular basis to help you. After you identify two errors, make a conscious effort to avoid them for at least two weeks.

    a. _____
    b. _____

2. When you are working on your motivational speech, create two of the following techniques to include in your speech.

    Metaphor: _____
    _____

    Simile: _____
    _____

    Repetition: _____
    _____

    Another form of figurative language: _____
    _____

References

123HelpMe.com. (2010, Jan. 5) *Anti Legalization of Marijuana In The Midst of a Drug Epidemic*. Retrieved from *http://www.123HelpMe.com/view.asp?id=131187*.

Aristotle's Rhetoric: Or, The True Grounds and Principles of Oratory; Showing the Right Art of Pleading and Speaking in Full Assemblies and Courts of Judicature. London: Robert Midgley, 1685.

Burton, G. O. (2001). The canons of rhetoric. *Silva Rhetoricae*. Retrieved from *http://rhetoric.byu.edu/canons/Canons.htm*

Cline, A. R. (2006). *Rhetorica: A rhetoric primer*. Retrieved from *http://rhetorica.net/textbook/index.htm*

Dombeck, M. (2005, Nov. 3). Transference. MentalHelp.net. Retrieved from *http://www.mentalhelp.net/poc/view_doc.php?type=doc&id=8253*

Dunn, T. (2003, Feb. 14). Nation copes with jitters. Disaster News Network. Retrieved from *http://www.disasternews.net/news/article.php?articleid=3021*

Forensics Community. (2009, Aug. 8). Excelling at declamation: An advanced guide. Retrieved from *http://www.forensicscommunity.com/declamation/excelling-declamation-advanced-guide*

Fortenbaugh, W. W. (2003). Theophrastean studies. Germany: Franz Steiner Verlag Stuttgart.

Golden, James L., Goodwin F. Berquist, William E. Coleman, Ruth Golden, and J. Michael Sproule (eds.). (2007). *The rhetoric of Western thought: From the Mediterranean world to the global setting*, 9th ed. Dubuque, IA (USA): p.67

Griffin, E. (2009). *A first look at communication theory*, 7th Ed. New York: McGraw-Hill.

Holguin, J. (2003, Jan. 5). *Fast food linked to child obesity.* Chicago: CBS News. Retrieved from http://www.cbsnews.com/stories/2004/01/05/ health/main591325.shtml.

Honeycutt, L. (2004). *Compiled resources. Aristotle's rhetoric.* Retrieved from *http://www.public.iastate.edu/~honeyl/Rhetoric/index.html*

Johnson, L. B. (1965, Mar. 15). "We shall overcome." Retrieved from *http://www.historyplace.com/speeches/johnson.htm*

Kennedy, J. F. (1961, Jan. 20). "Inaugural address." Retrieved from http://www.famousquotes.me.uk/speeches/John_F_Kennedy/5.htm

Lauer, J. M. (2004). Invention in rhetoric and composition. West Lafayette, IN: Parlor Press.

McCarthy, M. (2007). Renaissance and reformation Vol. VI. New York: White-Thomas Publishing.

Nixon, R. (1952, Sept. 23). "Checkers." Retrieved at *http://watergate. info/ nixon/checkers-speech.shtml*

Rapp, C. (2002, May 2). Aristotle's Rhetoric. Stanford Encyclopedia of Philosophy. Retrieved from http://plato.stanford.edu/entries/aristotle-rhetoric/

Salkind, N.J. (2007). *Statistics for people who (think they) hate statistics* 3rd ed. Thousand Oaks, CA: Sage.

Smith, M.C. (1950, June 1). "Declaration of Conscience." Retrieved from *http://www.americanrhetoric.com/speeches/margaretchasesmithconscience. html*

Vogel, S. (2007, Oct. 22). Teen driver menace: Text-messaging. Suite101. com. Retrieved from *http://parentingteens.suite101.com/ article.cfm/ teen_driver_menace_textmessaging.*

Winfrey, O. (2002, Sept. 22). 54th Annual EMMY Awards speech by Oprah Winfrey. Retrieved from *http://www.famousquotes.me.uk/ speeches/Oprah-Winfrey/index.htm.*

Chapter Three

Immediacy Behaviors and Delivery Techniques

The objectives of this chapter are to:

- ✓ Define Immediacy Behaviors.
- ✓ Compare Immediacy Behaviors as it Relates to Public Speaking Delivery.
- ✓ Comprehend How to Adapt to an Audience.
- ✓ Apply Immediacy Behaviors such as:

  - ➢ The Smile
  - ➢ Eye Contact
  - ➢ Displaying Warmth and an Open Posture
  - ➢ Proxemics
  - ➢ Messages that Cultivate Unity
  - ➢ Sincere Compliments
  - ➢ I Messages
  - ➢ Using Names
  - ➢ Personal Examples or Stories

Immediacy Behaviors Identified

Immediacy behaviors are behaviors that yield likeability. This is a powerful tool to a public speaker and to anyone who communicates with others. Virginia Richmond and James McCroskey (2000) define immediacy as "The degree of perceived physical or psychological closeness between people" (p. 212). Decades of research suggest that people who radiate immediacy behaviors display a sense of warmth that draws others to them. Teachers who display immediacy behaviors in the classroom are perceived as more understandable and provide students with a positive learning environment. People who display immediacy behaviors are more successful. These nonverbal and verbal cues enhance your ability to do well during a job interview and increase your likelihood of being promoted. The ideology of immediacy behaviors is discussed within this text to assist learners in enhancing their delivery skills in public address; however, making such behaviors a part of your overall interactions will improve your interpersonal relationships.

Think about the person in your life who you enjoy conversing with the most. Do not move on until you have this person in your mind. What are the characteristics of this person that draws you to her or him? Write the name and circle all that apply:

Name_____

- ○ Has a warm smile
- ○ Compliments me often
- ○ Is positive
- ○ Displays open posture

   o   Usually enjoys talking about topics that interest me
   o   Cares about me
   o   Believes that I am honest
   o   Enjoys my company
   o   Does not feel superior
   o   Calls me by the name that I prefer
   o   Makes me feel good about myself

The above traits and behaviors make people likeable. When you speak before a group of people, you should incorporate these same behaviors. Adept public speakers share delivery techniques that make them likeable and pull audiences to them because they enjoy listening. Immediacy behaviors are the characteristics that cause audiences to listen more closely. In the end, it is the delivery model that is welcoming and conversational in nature. Below is a self-report of Immediacy Behavior used with permission from Virginia Richmond.

Self-Report of Immediacy Behavior (SRIB)

Directions: Below are twelve statements that describe nonverbal behaviors that can lead to increased or decreased immediacy. Respond to each item on the five-point scale in the space provided. Presume that "5" means the statement is a very accurate description of how you typically behave in interpersonal encounters, and "1" means the statement is a very inaccurate description of your typical behavior in interpersonal encounters.

_____ 1.   I touch others when conversing with them.

_____ 2.   *I avoid eye contact when talking with others.

_____ 3.   *I move away from others when they touch me during a conversation.

_____ 4.   I sit or stand close to others during a conversation.

_____ 5.   *My voice is somewhat monotonous or dull when conversing with others.

_____ 6.   I frequently gesture while I talk to another person.

_____ 7.   I am very vocally animated when talking with others.

_____ 8.   I usually lean toward others when talking with them.

_____ 9.   *I seldom gesture while I talk to another person.

_____ 10.   I use a lot of eye contact when talking with others.

_____ 11.   *When others sit or stand close to me while conversing, I move away.

_____ 12.   *I usually lean away from others when talking with them.

Scoring Procedure

Step 1: Add responses to the items with an asterisk. _____

Step 2: Add responses to the items without an asterisk. _____

Step 3: Complete the following formula: SAI = (36 - Total of Step 1) + (Total of Step 2)

Interpretation of Score:

1. If your score is below 25, you probably are very non-immediate.
2. If your score is between 25 and 36, you probably are moderately non-immediate.
3. If your score is between 37 and 48, you probably are moderately immediate.
4. If you score is between 49 and 60, you probably are very immediate.

Smile

One way to increase likeability is to smile (Akiteng, 2008). A fake smile can cause you to appear phony, but causing yourself to think about positive things and to smile can brighten your mood (Cloud, 2009). Smiles that are insincere use only muscles around the mouth; whereas, genuine smiles engage the muscles around the eyes. Such smiles are contagious and make those around feel emotionally closer to the person smiling.

Although a smile is not always appropriate throughout your speech or conversation, you should smile during appropriate times to make your communication enjoyable. A speech that is depressing throughout will turn an audience away. Be positive when discussing any topic. Uplifting messages are preferred to using techniques such as scolding or depressing an audience. To establish meaningful connections, it is important to affirm others' self-worth. Consider a speech about adopting healthy lifestyles. It would be more persuasive to share amusing anecdotal stories about a person using extreme unhealthy habits rather than rebuking the audience. Then share specific, simple ways to change. Below is an example of a speech excerpt to encourage an audience to change unhealthy habits.

> *I am a huge fan of southern cooking. I learned to cook meals packed full of the main ingredients in southern cuisine such as lard. For those of you who do not remember lard, it is processed pig fat that is used in fluffy buttermilk biscuits and to fry foods such as chicken and potatoes. In previous decades, mothers everywhere purchased lard by the gallon. I can remember going to grandma's*

house and feasting on southern fried chicken, collard greens and ham hocks, mashed potatoes and sausage gravy, and a fried apple pie. Grandma always kept a paper towel roll on the table so we could keep the grease from rolling down our chins and arms. It was a cardiovascular episode waiting to happen; a delicious meal cooked with a gallon of pig fat, cholesterol, and love. I was so proud when I would watch my children enjoy such a meal. Afterward they would go into a comatose state as their digestive systems shifted into overdrive.

I still enjoy cooking for my family but omit lard and other fatty foods from my family's diet. Instead of pan fried chicken, I make oven fried chicken. Steamed vegetables are a tasty substitute for vegetables seasoned with ham hocks. A tasty dinner roll and a baked pie is a fine substitute for biscuits and fried pies. In the end, foods that allow you to enjoy the flavor and unique tastes are preferable to the battered and fried versions.

Although it is not appropriate to berate or put yourself or others down within a speech, laughing about your mistakes or an embarrassing faux pas is acceptable. As the nineteenth century poet, Ella Wheeler Wilcox wrote, "Laugh, and the world laughs with you; weep, and you weep alone" (Wallechinsky & Wallace, 1981). When you speak with or to others, make the event meaningful, yet enjoyable. Another quote by an unknown author gives us words to live by, "Don't take life too seriously, no one gets out alive." Being around people who cannot laugh and enjoy life robs us of hope. So smile and others will be enlivened by your presence.

Eye Contact

Books and articles that have been written about speech delivery include the immediacy behavior of making "good" eye contact. Eye contact is necessary for conversation and public speaking. However, eye contact is a learned behavior and the duration of eye contact varies within different cultures. American parents have taught their children to make eye contact but not to stare, because staring is rude in the American culture. As you walk down the halls at college or in a department store, you look at a person in the eye, nod, and then look away. If you are talking to an American and do not make eye contact, it will make you appear uninterested or dishonest. However, a person who was raised in Japan may become uneasy if you make eye contact (Richmond & McCroskey, 2000). Furthermore, in different countries around the globe, eye contact with a superior is a sign of disrespect. As we communicate with people of other cultures, it is important to learn about the meanings portrayed to them through our eyes.

Nonetheless, when communicating with people in the United States, eye contact is essential to connecting with your audience. Good eye contact is an ambiguous idea. Ridiculous advice has been given about how to appear to connect to the audience if a speaker has difficulty making eye contact. For example, authors have suggested that you look on the wall behind the audience, spanning back and forth, so it will seem that you are looking throughout the crowd. Spanning back and forth will only give your audience motion sickness, and they will look down or away to avoid this uncomfortable situation. Another suggestion is that you look at a spot on a person's shirt or at an audience member's forehead. If you stare at a woman's shirt, she may think that you have diverted your eyes to parts of her body that it is inappropriate to stare at. If you look at the foreheads of your audience, this could be a distraction. Those who do not feel comfortable looking at people in the eye need to break themselves of this, and look at people in the eye. This is not to stare. Make appropriate eye contact that is appropriate to the culture you are in.

Good eye contact in a speech comprises looking at a person in the audience in the eyes, finishing a thought or sentence, and then moving to another person in the audience. By the end of the speech, the speaker should connect with others throughout the room. It is similar to how an adept communicator converses in an everyday conversation with a group of friends. The eye contact made with others provides the speaker with positive connections to individuals.

When speaking with a diverse group, the speaker may look at an individual who looks down or away when eye contact is made. In this case, go to another member in the audience. It may be a cultural difference and not a sign that the person is being inattentive. Some people look away because they feel nervous and do not want to be singled out. Again, simply move to another person.

Public speaking causes anxiety for the majority of people around the world. Eye contact is unnerving if you feel uneasy. Remember that most of the people in your audience would be afraid if they were the ones in the front of the room. Therefore, the audience does not equate your nervousness with weakness. When you are presenting, you are the most respected individual in the room. You are the focal point, and you need to make a connection with your audience using a conversational delivery style.

The worst way to deliver a speech is by reading it. Reading a speech is boring and condescending. When I hear a speech that is read, I think, "Just give me your essay. I can read!" A speech that is conversational in nature provides a sense of emotional passion. When you look in the eyes of another person, you are reaching out to them. You express the nonverbal message that you care about your topic and that you want to relay this important information. This is what makes your presentation compelling and memorable. The only time that a speech should be read is if you have a teleprompter and your speech is a matter of national security. The president or a person giving a speech, in which the data must be precise, will read a speech that has been cleared through the proper channels. A speech of introduction is often read because of the need for the facts to be concise. Other than that, speeches should be delivered in an extemporaneous, conversational manner.

Looking at the audience provides speakers the opportunity to adapt to the audience. When giving a long speech or lecture, a speaker should use vocal variety and involve the audience with questions, activities, or discussions. Do not point out a dozing member the audience. Embarrassing people in an audience will reduce likeability.

I teach speech courses at a community college. I have students who walk into my classes every day who are juggling work, family, and school to better their lives. There are students who work night shifts and then come directly to class without rest so they can obtain a degree. It would be remiss to single out nodding students because they are tired. Instead, I provide students with fill-in-the-blank notes, walk around the room, and try to engage students when lecturing. It would be unfair to embarrass a student who has worked all night, and then nods off while finally sitting down during an hour and a half class. Eye contact with students engages them in the content. It also helps us to make an interpersonal connection. In the end, speeches and lectures are most effective when they connect the audience with the speaker via a conversational, pleasant speaking style.

Eye contact is audience contact. You should be comfortable enough with your topic and speech to discuss your ideas in a conversational setting. Walk to the lectern and place your notes on the lectern. Then simply talk to your audience as if they were your best friends. Do not consider your audience as naked or in their underwear, as some have suggested. Think of your audience as your best friends sitting on your couch at home. Talk to them as if they were all in a group, interested in your topic. Look one person in the eyes, complete a sentence, and then move to another audience member. Let your warm personality and passion show.

In conclusion, good eye contact is different depending on culture. Public speakers can use eye contact to enhance public speaking delivery by simply talking to their audiences about a topic that they care about. If an audience member looks away, move on. In the end, connect sincerely. Eye contact that is natural is the connection that pulls us together. Do not scan the room from side-to-side. Instead, look at an individual in the eye, move to another person, and connect with your audience as an endearing friend. That is good eye contact.

Displaying Warmth and an Open Posture

Imagine that you are at a party, and you want to mingle. There are two people that you look toward. One has a pleasant smile, is leaning slightly forward, appears relaxed, makes eye contact with you, and gives a friendly nod. The other person, is frowning slightly, arms are crossed, is leaning back slightly, makes little eye contact, and appears anxious, sad, or angry. The person displaying warm, open posture is the one that you will seek out to talk with. Open posture, eye contact, and a smile make the person appear available or open for conversation.

A public speaker should also display psychological availability to encourage an audience to listen. Open posture is important to hold the interest of your audience. We have been conditioned to avoid people with closed posture. Due to nervousness, however, public speakers may inadvertently display closed posture. Speakers who do not know what to do with their hands will clutch them, latch on to the lectern, or place them on their hips. I have seen nervous speakers hug themselves throughout a speech and even hug and sway. Such behaviors are distracting. To display open posture, watch the hands. Peter Watts (2009) wrote, "There are three things your hands should avoid touching during a presentation; your chest, your hips, and each other!" So what do we do with our hands?

The best speakers keep their hands toward the upper body while making natural gestures. Gesturing is not finger fidgeting or playing with items such as a ring, pen, or paper clip. Gestures are nonverbal cues that emphasize or complement the message. For example, if you have two points, you could say, "My first point . . ." while holding up one finger. This gives your audience a visual image that complements your verbal message. Your gestures should be normal for you and your personality. An animated communicator would have difficulty standing behind a lectern. However, some personalities do not lend themselves to great quantities of gesturing. Individuals who do not typically gesture in face-to-face communication should stand behind the lectern and relax their hands on the lectern. This is acceptable. Those who gesture frequently in everyday conversations will gesture frequently when in front of an audience.

When you move to the front of the room to give a presentation, be sure that you display open posture. Lay your notes and any other items down, stand with confidence keeping both feet on the floor, take a breath, smile, and begin with an attention grabber (see the motivational speech chapter for attention grabbing techniques). Look as confident as possible, even if you do not feel confident. Keep your presentation upbeat and sincere. Talk to your audience as you would to your best friend by being open and using the gestures that fit your personality. Keep both feet on the floor and stand up straight. If you lean on the lectern or a table or if you slouch, you are sending a nonverbal message that you are bored and uninterested in your message. In the end, skilled public speakers display warmth, confidence, and an open posture.

Proxemics

Proxemics is nonverbal communication that deals with the physical distance between people. It is the proximity that we are to a person when communicating. Acceptable distance varies between individuals and cultures. Edward Hall identified four spatial zones:

1. Intimate space   0–1½ feet
2. Personal space   1½–4 feet
3. Social space   4–12 feet
4. Public space   12 feet+ (Beebe, Beebe & Ivy, 2007)

When you move into intimate space with another person who does not want to be intimate with you, that person is likely to become uncomfortable and put up barriers. This is also known as invading the person's space. People who feel that their space has been violated will step back or cross their arms. However, if you stay within the social space zone with a close friend who prefers to be in your personal or intimate space, this may result in negative feelings. If you are talking to a friend or family member, give them your undivided attention, sit close, and lean forward. Within professional settings, personal to social space would be considered most appropriate. It is still important that you lean forward and be attentive. However, if there is any doubt about the proxemics comfort of a person you are communicating with, watch the nonverbal cues of the person or persons and adjust accordingly.

Public speakers often stand behind a lectern and even on a podium when addressing a group. The lectern and podium set the speaker apart from the audience, thus increasing the perception of proxemics. It may add a personable feel to a speech when the speaker moves closer to the audience. However, the speaker should not move into intimate space or the audience members will become uncomfortable. Each movement should be meaningful, and you should avoid pacing.

If you move from behind the lectern toward your audience, choose the right time. For instance, you may want to move toward the center of the audience when you tell a story. At this time, you may lean forward and use more gestures. Then you could move to the right when you bring up a new point, and move to the left when you are elaborating on a point. The movement should be deliberate and meaningful. A speaker who emits a natural, friendly style may get away with moving up an aisle, but pacing up and down the aisle causes your audience to be uncomfortable, especially if they are trying to keep up with you. It will make you appear stiff if you choreograph every move. However, if you plan to move away from the lectern, make the movement meaningful and comfortable for the audience.

I enjoy lecturing and am animated. It is difficult for me when I must stand behind a lectern throughout, even if it is a five-minute presentation. I am cautious to move in a meaningful way. I tend to stay to the left of a room, so I purposefully move to the right front of my classroom when shifting to another point. After I have spent weeks with students, I will sometimes move closer and talk to individuals. This works to wake them up. I ask questions to individuals only if I believe that it will not embarrass them and that the student knows the answer to the question. Because I enjoy speaking so much, I make an effort to ask open-ended discussion questions. At the beginning of a class, I stay to the front of the room. As I get to know my students, I move closer to them during lectures or discussions.

Proxemics communicates nonverbal messages to others. If we violate personal space, it will make others uncomfortable. If we do not sit close and lean toward a person we are communicating with, we appear standoffish or unfriendly. Those who feel comfortable moving away from the lectern when speaking may add a personable atmosphere to a presentation. In the end, your movements and proximity to the audience should enhance the presentation, not distract from your message or make the audience feel uncomfortable.

Messages That Cultivate Unity

Immediacy messages relay a sense of belonging. These messages include statements such as "we," rather than "me." When communicating to one person or a group of people, use words and phrases that cultivate unity. Words or phrases that place you with the audience are preferable. Review the excerpt from Franklin Roosevelt's "First inaugural address."

> *We* are stricken by no plague of locusts. Compared with the perils which *our* forefathers conquered, because they believed and were not afraid, *we* have still much to be thankful for. Nature still offers her bounty and human efforts have multiplied it. Plenty is at *our* doorstep, but a generous use of it languishes in the very sight of the supply.

Throughout the speech, he uses powerful language that fosters unity. Additional verbal immediacy techniques include expressing warmth, self-disclosure, and identification. Expressions of warmth include words of empathy and caring: "I understand why you are angry," "You are important to me," "We are in this together." Statements that are accusatory will cause a listener to turn attention away and put up defensive barriers.

Self-disclosure is simply sharing information about you. You do not want to share information that would be inappropriate, but share information about yourself that others can identify with. Bacal (2009) offers advice about getting through barriers through self-disclosure. "When speaking to groups (keynotes, meetings, speeches, public speaking), it's always a good tactic to share a little of yourself as a person, so you can overcome depersonalization barriers to group communication" (Bacal & Associates, 2009, par. 4). The right amounts of self-disclosure when speaking to a group is what humanizes you to an audience.

Identification aligns a speaker with listeners by showing common ground. Stephen Lucas (2009) defined identification as, "A process in which speakers seek to create a bond with the audience by emphasizing common values, goals, and experiences" (p. 97). To identify with an audience, you must understand the audience and point out commonalities. President Barack Obama (2009) delivered a compelling speech when he accepted his Nobel Peace Prize. Even his most ardent critics applauded this speech. It is one example of a presentation that uses verbal immediacy to establish identification.

> *Somewhere today, in the here and now, in the world as it is, a soldier sees he's outgunned, but stands firm to keep the peace. Somewhere today, in this world, a young protestor awaits the brutality of her government, but has the courage to march on. Somewhere today, a mother facing punishing poverty still takes the time to teach her child, scrapes together what few coins she has to send that child to school—because she believes that a cruel world still has a place for that child's dreams.*
>
> *Let us live by their example.*

This speech echoes the hopes of humankind. Such words show a middle ground that we share. Pointing out such common ground is how you establish identification.

In summary, verbal immediacy messages cultivate warmth and likeability. Techniques include pronouns such as we and our, and words that express empathy and caring. Appropriate self-disclosure provides your audience with information about you that emphasizes similar experiences. Identification creates a bond with your audience by showing commonalities. Another verbal immediacy technique is the use of sincere compliments.

Sincere Compliments

Peter Harris (2006) suggests that the number one reason that marriages fail is poor communication. Additional research suggests that positive, affirming communication provides people in relationships with optimal outcomes that allow them to achieve their ideal selves. The Michelangelo phenomenon is a relationship model where another person enhances her or his partner's self-worth, and thereby enhances the relationship. "Numerous studies have revealed that partner enhancement is beneficial to individuals and to relationships: For example, when partners perceive one another more positively than each person perceives himself or herself, relationships exhibit superior functioning" (Rusbult, Finkel, & Kumashiro, 2009). To maintain a healthy relationship, it is important to consistently affirm the other person's sense of self-worth.

A person who is likeable affirms others' self-esteem by using sincere compliments. In other words, a person who is likeable causes others to feel good about themselves. Think about the person who is consistently joking at other people's expense. It may be funny occasionally, but most people will not want to spend vast quantities of time with the consistent heckler. For mental well-being, people will steer clear of critical, closed-minded, pessimistic people. If you must be around this type of person, you want to spend the least amount of time with such a person as possible. Communication with open-minded, optimistic people is enjoyable and uplifting. It is okay to have differing views, but there is no need to get angry or become critical, if someone has a different belief. Such criticism and unwarranted anger causes pain in any relationship. The pleasure gleaned from a relationship must exceed the punishment or the relationship will deteriorate (Devito, 2008).

When conflict occurs in a relationship, it is important that the parties continue to affirm the other's self-esteem or the result will be detrimental to the relationship. You can wear people down by nagging or condemning another person. You may get your way for the short term, but when partners are not affirming each other, the relationship will not last. Relationships erosion has been blamed on problems with money, sexual incompatibility, abuse, jealousy, etc. However, the underlying issue is still that the self-worth of another was not affirmed. It is important to any relationship that people give the other specific, sincere compliments, listen to the goals of their partner or friend, and be positive, not judgmental, or insulting.

This important immediacy behavior is also valuable for the public speaker. Sincerely complimenting an audience member cultivates feelings of goodwill to the speaker. The compliment must be sincere as opposed to empty flattery. Furthermore, it is never appropriate to insult a person in an audience, and this includes in the classroom. "Praise in public and punish in private" (Business Intelligence Lowdown, 2007). I was in a college class where the professor insulted a student. At the end of the class, students huddled outside and talked about how unfair the professor was. The class bonded because they shared a common enemy. It is doubtful that students in the class listened or learned from this professor. It is difficult to listen to someone that you do not like or respect. Can you think of a college professor or high school teacher that you disliked? Did you feel that you learned something from this person? A person that has insulted one member of the audience has made an enemy of many people in the audience. You do not listen to your enemy. If you must hear a person you do not like or trust speak, you do not listen. Instead, all that you hear is stupidity coming out of her or his mouth. You take the words and skew them in such a way that they make the sender of the message appear ridiculous in your mind. He or she may be relaying profound information, but you will not hear it the way in which it was sent. Therefore, keep your audience with you and do not do anything that would be insulting or offensive.

A compliment should be sincere or heartfelt. It should also be specific and typically about some attribute or action that the person can control. It should not be something that could embarrass the person or be construed as sexual harassment. You should compliment people for good service. For example, "I appreciate the good service you offered today, Lisa. You had our coffee cups filled before they were half-empty, and you have such a warm smile." A public speaker might say something like, "When I arrived this evening, I was greeted by Larry. He made me feel right at home by showing me around and introducing me to others. Larry, I appreciate your high level of professionalism."

Sincere compliments should be part of your everyday conversations and be used during a speech. You will not accomplish much by insulting or scolding others. Instead, be positive and offer a sincere compliment when you can. During your next conversation, try giving a heartfelt compliment. Before your next public speech, talk to someone in the audience and provide a positive remark to that person. Share your dreams and aspirations with others and let them express themselves to you. Receive a compliment by simply saying, "Thank you." Foster a climate of acceptance wherever you are.

I Messages

Adept communicators take responsibility for their behaviors and emotions. Another person cannot make you feel anything. Your feelings and behaviors are yours and are developed because of your personal frame of reference. The way you perceive a situation is based on your experiences, ideologies, beliefs, and values. What affirms self-worth varies from one person to the next, and what would anger one person will vary from what would disgust or upset another person. For example, a woman who has been taught that a hug is a sign of intimacy between partners may become upset if another woman were to hug her husband. The husband and female friend may view this as an act of innocent friendship, while the wife looks on in horror. Conversely, a person who is a hugger would not perceive such an event as offensive but as platonic as a handshake.

Beebe, Beebe & Ivy (2007) defined an "I" message as, "A message in which you state your perspective or point of view" (p. 272). And a "you" message as, "A message that is likely to create defensiveness in others because it emphasizes how another person has created a problem, rather than describing the problem from one's own perspective" (Beebe, Beebe & Ivy, 2007, p. 272). In the above example, discussing the issue with a "you" message would cause the husband to be defensive as the wife said something like, "You make me so mad when you grope on other women. Who is she?" An "I" message would work to discuss the problem positively. Wait to express how you feel when you are alone and are calm. Then, the conversation can be discussed without putting the other person on defensive mode. For example, "I was taught that hugs are to be displayed for intimacy. I realize that you do not want to upset me, but I feel insecure when you hug another woman. In the future, let's keep hugs among us."

When using "I" messages, describe the emotion that you are experiencing, taking responsibility for your emotion without blaming the other person for causing you this emotion. I described the use of "I" messages in one of my classes and asked students to try this in a communication event. One of my students wrote about how this assisted her in a situation that could have erupted into an argument but ended up improving her and her husband's relationship.

She wrote about a time when she and her husband were eating out with a group of friends. Her husband told everyone at the table that his wife snored so loud that she shook the windows in their home. The people at the table laughed as the wife became furious about his making fun of her and revealing what she perceived to be a disgusting, uncontrollable behavior. She made the wise decision to not bring this up in front of the group, but waited to discuss it in the privacy of their home. By the time they arrived home, she had calmed down. Then she said, "I felt embarrassed when you told our friends about my snoring. My mother used to say that snoring was not very ladylike. I cannot control my snoring. Because of the way I was raised, I don't want my friends to know that I snore. In the future, could we let this be our little secret?" Her husband's response was, "I am sorry. I didn't realize." "I" messages allow others to strengthen their relationships, whereas "you" messages have caused long arguments that hurl blame and hurtful comments.

When publicly addressing an audience, the speaker can discuss ideologies based upon her personal frame of reference and how these views may be different than others. It is okay to bring up the opposing view and explain your meaning. Martin Luther King Jr. used powerful "I" messages in his "I Have a Dream" speech. It is a speech that utilizes

"I" messages by describing a hope that caring individuals can identify with.

If you become angry with another person, take a breath and consider what you will say before you hurl hurtful comments. Take responsibility for your emotions. As a public speaker, realize that the message that you send your audience is coming from your frame of reference, and is being filtered through their frames of reference. Use caution to not say words that would cause any person to be defensive. Bring up the differences and celebrate your commonalities.

Using Names

In general, people are egocentric. We like to talk about ourselves and for others to positively talk about us. When speaking to an audience, focus on the audience. Let your audience know how your presentation will positively affect their lives. You should have conducted some sort of audience analysis. It is good to talk to people before you present to discover interests. Use this information within the speech if possible. Also, slide in names of audience members. When I teach, I will say a student name. For example, "Terry, did you know that listening is the most used communication skill? Have you had any courses over the years on listening? Most people have not." I would know Terry enough to realize that this would not embarrass her. But using a name every once in a while will focus the audience.

Your name is the most important word to you. When communicating with others, you should use a person's name when possible (Carnegie, 1981). Work diligently to learn and remember the names of people you work with. It is difficult for me to remember about 165 students per semester, but I make an effort to memorize names as soon as I can. It is also important to call people by their preferred name and to pronounce names correctly. Dale Carnegie explains the importance of a name:

> We should be aware of the magic contained in a name and realize that this single item is wholly and completely owned by the person with whom we are dealing . . . and nobody else. The name sets the individual apart; it makes him or her unique among all others. The information we are imparting or the quest we are making takes on a special

importance when we approach the situation with the name
of the individual. From the waitress to the senior executive,
the name will work magic as we deal with others. (Carnegie,
1981, p. 83)

When you are communicating with people or in front of an
audience, use people's names when possible. When you are speaking to
a group over the course of time such as employees or students, use their
names. You do not want to single anyone out to embarrass them, but
use this as a communication tool that will help you connect with others.

Personal Examples or Stories

From the attention grabber to the conclusion, personal examples
and stories make you appear genuine, approachable, and likeable. It is
important that you tell a story with enthusiasm or drama. The story can
be hypothetical or real, just as long as it is memorable. I heard a speech
with this hypothetical story at the beginning.

> *Imagine that you are at your family reunion. Everyone is feasting
> on fried chicken, pork ribs, mashed potatoes, roast beef,
> biscuits, and corn on the cob. Then tragedy strikes. Aunt Marie
> starts choking on a rib bone. What are you going to do? Hopefully,
> someone in the crowd has been trained in first aid and CPR. That
> person should be you.*

The story allows the audience members to visualize a situation
when they may need to know first aid and CPR. He told it with such
animation and explained the family reunion in even more detail that it
was amusing and enjoyable. He also brought us back to the hypothetical
situation at the end of the speech, describing how you saved Aunt Marie
and became the family hero.

The most moving speeches use personal stories. These heartfelt
or amusing stories and examples allow your audience to vicariously
experience an event. Statistics and other forms of data are important
when establishing a need or a cause, but too much of this kind of
information makes the speech boring and unmemorable. Read the
speech "Letting go" at the end of the chapter. This starts with a story

and completes the story at the end. Then there are personal illustrations and examples throughout. In the end, personal stories are personal to you and add a personable touch to your presentation.

Before and After the Presentation

When you are presenting for the first time, you need to ask questions about the room, the equipment, and the audience. Ask how many people are going to be there and the size of the room. Your audience size should match the room size. If you show up in a large room with few people, ask the people to move to the front of the room. If there are more people than there are seats available, have seats brought in. Begin your speech after everyone is seated comfortably.

Ask about the equipment. If you have a PowerPoint or Prezi presentation, ask what type of computer and projector will be available. Do not assume that the computer will be connected to the Internet or that it will provide enough sound for a video. Ask about audio speakers and Internet connections. Always send your presentation and presentation aids to yourself through e-mail and bring your presentation and presentation aids on a jump drive. It is good to have a laptop backup if that is possible, and even a hard copy of all documents would be additional backup. Print out all documents and PowerPoint slides. Place a copy of all PowerPoint slides in front of you so you do not need to look at the screen when presenting.

Ask if a microphone is available and what kind of microphone will be provided. If you are a person whose hands shake, ask for a microphone stand or preferably a lavalier microphone which is a lapel microphone. Lavaliers are best if you like to move around. If you are provided a microphone, use it. It provides you the ability to speak in a natural tone without yelling at your audience. If you do not feel comfortable using a microphone, use it anyway. I will not use a handheld microphone because I am a shaker and it causes a distraction for me and the audience, and a shaking microphone makes nervousness noticeable. I was presenting an award one day and did not realize I was nervous, until I looked down and saw that my handheld microphone and a piece of paper were shaking in my hands. This moved my emotions from a little anxious streak to a freak-out mode. I then tried to steady the microphone on my chin, but this caused the microphone to rattle on my teeth. The sound over the loudspeakers was not pleasant. I ended up saying the wrong name of the person receiving the award and then rambled on with other misinformation. Later, I was told that no one cared but me. Although I thought it was the end of the world, no one remembers that day but me and probably the person who received the award. If I am nervous, I avoid handheld microphones or holding papers in my hands when presenting.

You should also learn as much about the audience as possible. Ask about age, occupation, and gender. Also find out if children will be in the audience and any other relevant information. In other words, conduct an audience analysis before you arrive. Arrive early to give yourself time to set up and to talk to as many people as you can. Learn names and interests. Let them talk about themselves. Learn about individuals so you can adapt your speech according to their needs. You will not have time to rewrite your notes, but think of things that you could add that might make it more memorable for the specific audience. Remember a sincere compliment or the use of a name could be helpful.

After the presentation, wait to pack up. You should talk to the people in the audience. It is also helpful to provide anonymous evaluation sheets. Ask for any feedback that you can use to assist you in future presentations. It would be helpful if someone would video tape you presenting at least a few times. You learn volumes about your presentation delivery by watching yourself on video. Be open to suggestions about how you can improve. Do not ask overly critical people their advice. I usually ask students in my classes to comment on the most valuable thing that they learned, the most frustrating thing about the class, and what the instructor could do to improve the course. Below is an example of a more in-depth evaluation form that was created by a colleague, Dr. Rick Merritt. You would edit the evaluation form based on the purpose of your presentation.

Workshop Evaluation Form

Name (Optional):
E-mail (Optional):

The goal of this workshop was to present a practical method of giving a persuasive presentation. Please rate this workshop using the following scale.

The information presented will assist me in preparing effective presentations.

Strongly Disagree	Disagree	Neutral	Agree	Strongly Agree
1	2	3	4	5

The activities were effective in reinforcing the subject matter.

Strongly Disagree	Disagree	Neutral	Agree	Strongly Agree
1	2	3	4	5

The information provided in the handouts will be useful to me.

Strongly Disagree	Disagree	Neutral	Agree	Strongly Agree
1	2	3	4	5

The instructor is knowledgeable about the subject area.

Strongly Disagree	Disagree	Neutral	Agree	Strongly Agree
1	2	3	4	5

The instructors demonstrated excellent presentation skills.

Strongly Disagree	Disagree	Neutral	Agree	Strongly Agree
1	2	3	4	5

I would recommend this workshop to my colleagues.

Strongly Disagree	Disagree	Neutral	Agree	Strongly Agree
1	2	3	4	5

This workshop was an effective use of my time.

Strongly Disagree	Disagree	Neutral	Agree	Strongly Agree
1	2	3	4	5

Your comments or any recommendations that you might have to improve *any* aspect of our future professional development workshops are welcome.

We welcome comments about what we should continue in future workshops.

When presenting, go early and stay late. Gather information about the situation and the audience before you present. Technology can be helpful if it is used correctly and if it functions as planned. Always have a backup plan. Before you speak, meet with as many of the people in the audience as possible. Make sure everyone is comfortable and settled in before you begin. Afterward, allow time for meaningful feedback, and be open to improvements.

Summary

Decades of research would suggest that immediacy behaviors in the classroom increases student learning. Immediacy behaviors increase audience understanding, speaker credibility, and speaker likeability. The ability to display immediacy behaviors is important in a variety of speaking situations such as lectures, workshops, interviews, sales presentations, motivational speeches, and when conducting meetings. Immediacy behaviors are valuable tools to enhance relationships as well as speaking delivery techniques. Nonverbal immediacy behaviors include a warm smile, eye contact, open posture, and proxemics. Verbal immediacy behaviors include use of words that denote unity, warmth, self-disclosure, identification, sincere compliments, "I" messages, and use of names, personal stories, and examples. It is also important to conduct situational and demographical audience analysis when speaking with a group. Go early and meet people. Also, obtain feedback after you have presented.

Assessing Immediacy Behaviors

On a scale of one to five with one being the least and five being the greatest, rate your immediacy behaviors. For any behaviors that you give yourself a score below a four, write a specific plan to improve on this behavior. This would include the weakness and a specific plan to improve. For example, I do not always smile when I begin a speech. This may be because I feel rushed. In the future, I will make a concerted effort to place items on the lectern, get situated, take a breath, look at my audience, and smile before beginning my presentation.

An example of improving immediacy behaviors in relationships could include: Sometimes I inadvertently display closed posture when talking with others that I do not know well. During the next three times that I am in this situation, I am going to work toward using open posture. I will sit closer to the person, lean forward, maintain appropriate eye contact, smile, and ask questions that will encourage the person to talk about herself.

____ 1. Warm Smile

_____

_____

_____

____ 2. Eye Contact

_____

_____

_____

____ 3. Open Posture

_____

_____

_____

____ 4. Proxemics

_____

_____

_____

___ 5. Words That Denote Unity

_____

_____

_____

___ 6. Self-Disclosure

_____

_____

_____

___ 7. Identification

_____

_____

_____

___ 8. Sincere Compliments

_____

_____

_____

___ 9. "I" Messages

_____

_____

_____

___ 10. Using Names

_____

_____

_____

Letting Go

Introduction

I. (Attention) The fact that things will change is one of the few things in this life that we can depend on. All of us have had to alter our plans, step away from what makes us comfortable, and make changes in our lives and relationships. Change is difficult, especially if we are tenaciously holding on to what we must eventually let go of.
II. Rosanne Cash wrote, "The key to change is to let go of fear."
III. (Preview) Today, I would like to tell you about a time when I had to change. If I had let go of the past sooner, it would have saved me much heartache. I hope you can learn from my mistakes as you make daily adjustments toward a promising future.

Body

I. When my oldest daughter was fourteen, we were having one of those conversations that parents live for. I was imparting words of moral wisdom that I thought was oozing into the fibers of her being.

   A. Then she pulled out a spoiler bomb, and ruined everything. She looked at me intently in the face and asked, "Mom, have you ever lied to me?"
   B. I placed my finger on my lip, my thumb under my chin, and looked down in a gesture that would communicate that I really needed to think about this question. All the while I was thinking, why was she asking me this question? It must be a trick. After all, when I ask her if she is lying, I already know that she is.

II.   Doesn't she remember the times when I felt compelled to stretch, bend, and break the truth to protect her? Like when she had her first experience with death.

    A.   She was four and her sister was three. We were visiting a feed store where there were baby ducks in a pen. I made a terrible decision to buy five baby ducks. After bringing them home, we put the darlings in a bathtub of water. The phone rang, and while I was talking, my four-year-old daughter started screaming that the ducks were swimming funnily. I tried to assure her that ducks love water and are born excellent swimmers. She insisted that I needed to check on the ducks and so I hung up the phone and went to the bathroom. The babies were swimming funnily, with their heads underwater. I did not know that ducks could drown.

    B.   I picked up all of the ducks and put them in a towel. It was obvious that three were already dead, and two were cold, and might not make it. Quickly, I put my oldest on the couch and asked her to stay there for a few minutes, while I helped the baby ducks.

    C.   Then, I wrapped the three dead ducks in a newspaper and placed the other two in front of the bathroom heater. Finally, I ran out the backdoor to the large, green trash can and threw the deceased ducks inside.

    D.   "Where are my ducks?" my daughter sobbed. "Two of them are in the bathroom getting warm." I answered. She was not satisfied. "Where are the other three?" I told her that they were in ducky heaven. Surprisingly, this pacified the little girl as visions of her ducks waddling down streets of gold in ducky heaven floated across her mind.

        (a)   Then my three-year-old announced, "No, they are not! Those ducks are dead and Mommy threw them in the big trash can. They are right outside in the big trashcan. Gee!"

        (b)   My oldest swooned in shock, and I was speechless. My three-year-old daughter had played her typical role of investigator and could not understand the cover-up. The ducks were dead and in the trash—gee!

III. Then I realized that my daughter who had reached her teenage years did not remember the times that I lied to protect her and me. But now things were changing.

A. In those days I was the mommy goddess.
B. In those wonderful days of my life I knew all, had eyes that could see all, and I could eradicate every monster hiding in closets and under beds with my magic water.

IV. Now, things were changing. At fourteen, she didn't need the mommy goddess anymore. We were moving toward another type of relationship that was unexplored.

A. As my children grew, they needed a mother that they could confide in. The monsters were more complex so that the mommy magic could not destroy them. As my children grew, they needed me to disclose my weaknesses so they could disclose theirs.
B. It was time to change, to treat my children as intelligent people, to admit that I made mistakes, and that I understood that they made mistakes as well.
C. This was a time when they needed to comprehend that I was not perfect but human.

V. At that point of realization, I put my hand away from my face into my lap. Then I looked my daughter in the eye and answered her question with, "Hmm. Not that I can remember."
VI. Because, at that point in time, I was not ready to change. I liked being on the mommy pedestal.

A. It took about three more years full of fighting for her to finally knock me off that mommy goddess pedestal. She knew that I made mistakes and pointed every one out until I finally decided to let go and move on.
B. When I finally got off the pedestal, I discovered that the change wasn't so bad. The face-to-face view was what we both needed. I would have eliminated so much pain if I had simply given in to the change three years prior.

Conclusion

I.   In conclusion, it is uncomfortable to adapt to changing times, relationships, and careers.

II. Rosanna Cash understood this when she said that, "The key to change is to let go of fear."

III. Change is the only thing that you can depend on, so learn to adapt to the changes that are before you.

IV. Let go and embrace change, or brace yourself. If you do not give way to change, it will happen with or without your consent. You can ride it as the captain of your life or flail upstream until you give way . . . or drown in stagnancy.

References

Akiteng, Y. C. (2008, April 18). *How likable are you? Your smile says a lot. Ezine Articles.* Retrieved from *http://ezinearticles. com/?How-Likable-Are-You?-Your-Smile-Says-A-Lot&id=1118838*

Bacal & Associates. (2009). Disclosure as a communication tool. *Communication Resource Center.* Retrieved from http://work911.com/ communication/skillselfdisclosure.htm

Beebe, S. A., Beebe, S. J. and Ivy, D. K. (2007). *Communication: Principles for a lifetime.* Boston, Massachusetts: Allyn and Bacon.

Business Intelligence Lowdown. (2007, Feb 22). *How to be a manager that your employees respect: 73 surefire tips.* Retrieved from *http://www. businessintelligencelowdown.com/2007/02/how_to_be_a_man.html*

Carnegie, D. (1981). *How to win friends and influence people.* New York: Pocket Books.

Cloud, J. (2009, Jan. 19). *How to lift your mood? Try smiling. Time.* Retrieved from *http://www.time.com/time/health/article/0,8599, 1871687,00.html*

Devito, J. (2008). *Human communication: The basic course.* Boston, Massachusetts: Allyn and Bacon.

Lucas, S. E. (2009). *The art of public speaking*, 10th ed. Boston, Massachusetts: McGraw Hill.

Harris, P. (2006, Sept. 5). *The number one reason why most marriages fail.* EzineArticles.com. Retrieved from *http://ezinearticles.com/? The-Number-One-Reason-Why-Most-Marriages-Fail&id=1471057*

King, M. L. (1963, Aug. 28). "I Have a Dream." Analyzed by Peterson, J. A. in 2005. *Speech Topics Help.* Retrieved from *http://www. speech-topics-help.com/i-have-a-dream-speech.html*

Mehrabian, A. (2009). *Nonverbal communication*. Piscataway, NJ: Aldine Transaction.

Obama, B. (2009, Dec. 10). "Obama's Nobel Peace Prize Speech." *Chicago Sun-Times.*

O'Brien, L. (2009). *A speaker's resource: Listener-centered public speaking.* Boston: McGraw Hill.

Pausch, R. (2007, Sept. 18). "Really Achieving Your Childhood Dreams." Retrieved from http://download.srv.cs.cmu.edu/~pausch/Randy/pauschlastlecturetranscript.pdf

Roosevelt, F. D. (1933, March 4). "First Inaugural Address." *American Rhetoric: Top 100 Speeches.* Retrievedfromhttp://www.americanrhetoric. com/speeches/fdrfirstinaugural.html.

Rubinstein, B.B. (1970). Language Within Language: Immediacy, a Channel in Verbal Communication: By Morton Wiener and Albert Mehrabian. New York: Appleton-Century-Crofts, 1968. 214 pp. Psychoanal Q., 39:489–493.

Rusbult, C., Finkel, E. J., and Kumashiro, M. (2009, June 30). The Michelangelo phenomenon. Retrieved from *http:// faculty.wcas. northwestern.edu/eli-finkel/documents/55_RusbultFinkelKumashiroInPress_CDir.pdf.*

Wallenchinsky, D. and Wallace, I. (1981). Origins of sayings: Laugh and the world laughs with you. *Trivia-Library.com.* Retrieved from *http:// www.trivia-library.com/b/origins-of-sayings-laugh-and-the-world-laughs- with-you.htm*

Watts, P. (2009, April 27). Presentation body language: Hands and open posture. *The Presenters' Blog.* Retrieved from http://speak2all.wordpress.com/2009/04/27/presentation-body-language-hands-and- open-posture/

Chapter Four

Storytelling

The objectives of this chapter are to:

- ✓ Understand the need for effective storytelling.
- ✓ Differentiate why and when to tell a story.
- ✓ Understand how to prepare for a story
- ✓ Developing the elements of a good story
- ✓ A setting from which the audience understands and relates
- ✓ Interesting main characters
- ✓ Starting with a meaningful hook
- ✓ Developing conflict
- ✓ Providing a surprise ending.
- ✓ Differentiate effects of oral storytelling versus written stories.
- ✓ Examine the benefits of memorable and positive language.
- ✓ Explain the use of adaptation, visuals, and body language when telling a story.

I was on a plane from Honolulu to Phoenix. A man in the aisle across from me was smartly dressed and spoke with the woman next to him in a captivating, animated fashion. Although I could not hear much of the conversation, I was fascinated by the way the man spoke. He was an obviously remarkable storyteller who captured and held the attention of a stranger for six hours.

It was at that time that I began pondering the importance of storytelling in speeches, lectures, sales presentations, and any other situations in which one would want the attention of another human being. The better we are at storytelling, the better we can relay information that is easier to retain.

Storytelling has been used throughout time. Although it is uncertain when it began, it is believed that storytelling was a way to pass on history before mankind could write. Stories were first recorded as art on cave walls. Today, stories are still enjoyed in speeches, books, movies, plays, conversations, advertisements, and so on. The best storytellers are animated, use vivid language, and present meaningful, lively stories. This chapter is designed to explain the art of storytelling.

Why Tell a Story?

Researchers suggest that storytelling is "the most powerful means of communicating a message" (Gottschall, 2012, p. 1). Storytelling is a way to stir emotions in order to influence employees, sell a product, develop an image, motivate a student, challenge an audience, encourage a friend, get colleagues to go along with a corporate change, or gain donors.

Psychologists have discovered that the more one is drawn into a story, the more a story changes the audience member or reader (Gottschall, 2012). In fact, people who are moved by a story will often overlook fallacies that exist. People are much more likely to be influenced by a story than by facts. Because humans love stories so much, it is a good way to appeal to an audience who may not agree with a topic.

Gottschall (2012) wrote the book, *The Storytelling Animal: How Stories Make Us Human.* He suggests that storytelling is a way that we share the experiences of life that connect us as human beings. By telling a story, the storytellers brings other human beings to a life-changing event that the audience can identify with; it connects us. "But we are beasts of emotion more than logic. We are creatures of story, and the process of changing one mind or the whole world must begin with 'Once upon a time'" (Gottschall, 2012, par. 11).

A well-spoken story can yield much higher results than statistics on a PowerPoint. I dissuade students' use of PowerPoint or Prezi presentations when telling stories in class. Showing a picture of a person in your story could work, but the best stories interlace vivid imagery and compelling plots and characters. You have conflict and describe how the protagonist perseveres to survive. "All great storytellers since the dawn of time—from the ancient Greeks through Shakespeare and up to the present day—have dealt with this fundamental conflict between subjective expectation and cruel reality" (McKee and Fryer, 2014, par. 7). How do you spark innovative ideas for storytelling?

Preparing for the Story

The first key to storytelling is knowing your audience. I heard a storyteller address a group of college students with stories that would have been great for second graders. As any time you speak, know your audience and prepare your presentation for that audience. Consider age, gender, interests, and intellectual level of the audience. Listen and read stories of others that entertain, inspire, and move audience.

If possible, discover the interests, passions, dreams, and concerns of your audience. Do you have a story that will help your audience follow their dreams or overcome their fears?

Another thing to consider when preparing a story is audience bias. There are many people who cannot listen to a speaker if that speaker does not vote the same way that they do or that person does not have the same beliefs. Therefore, it is important to consider your audience's biases so that you will not offend and impede their ability to listen.

There are many stories already written that you can use as examples. However, when I am telling a story, I use examples from my life. I have written down stories to help me remember things that have happened in my life. Keeping a journal of entertaining events will help you remember these examples when you present. There are also amusing events that have happened that you share in everyday conversations that can make their way to your presentations. Think about stories you have told or others have told you that have been entertaining. Then think of ways that you can relay those stories better and to make a point.

Elements of a Good Story

A setting from which the audience understands and relates

In telling stories, situate your audience in a setting that is complete with a background and foreground. In science-fictional stories, the author usually spends a great deal of time developing the setting. An everyday setting will not need as many details, but provide sensory details. Let your audience know how it sounds, feels, tastes, looks, and smells to be in your story. Are the surroundings picturesque, charming, damp, gloomy, brilliant, bitter, musty, crisp, and so on? Use figurative language to give a more intense view of the setting.

An interesting main character(s)

To capture an audience, you need a compelling story line and a hero/heroine. Within a presentation, keep the number of characters in the story to a minimum or the audience will become confused. The main character need not be beautiful or even nice. The character should be someone or something that we want to love or love to hate. The audience needs to be able to see the world through the protagonist's frame of reference. Vividly and passionately put your audience in the mind and heart of the protagonist.

You may be the protagonist of your story, or it may be a real or made-up character. Either way, permit your audience to understand the character as a relatable character. Even your hero will have faults or shortcomings to overcome. Oftentimes, the weaknesses and need to change make the character(s) interesting and one in which the audience can connect.

One of my favorite characters in a book is Alex Cross. In the *Alex Cross* series, James Patterson tells the story inside the mind and life of Alex Cross, and then you experience the plot from inside the mind and experience of the antagonist or criminal.

When you develop a story, consider your personal heroes. You may be the hero in that you are the person who has overcome adversity. Now you have the tools to help others pave a similar successful path.

Start with a meaningful, unexpected hook

Read the first paragraph of any novel. Good writers know how to pull in an audience with an unexpected twist at the very beginning. The first few lines of the story should be gripping. Begin with a vivid depiction of a scene or start the story with a mystery or just ask a provocative question. Let your opening lines set the tone and the mood for the story.

Conflict

A story is not worth telling without conflict. The hero of the story may be facing a moral dilemma, hardship, antagonist, deep sorrow, or paradigm shift. The creator of the conflict may be the fault of another person, society, death or illness, or even the fault of the main character. The conflict may be excruciatingly painful, amazingly life changing, or irresistibly amusing, but the story is birthed out of conflict.

The ending

The story needs a surprise ending. If a story is predictable, the audience will not want to follow all the way through. You do not need to signal the ending, but it should be obvious you are coming to a close. You will reach a climatic point or high point of the story, and then the events after the climax will close the story.

Oral storytelling

Orally telling a story should intensify the emotions. One can hear the sounds, smells, beauty, savagery, angst, anguish, passions, elation, relief, and so on, through the words and nonverbal cues. The speaker needs to have the passion, emotion, and the appropriate amount of gestures to bring an audience through the wiles of an effective story. Your reason for telling your story influences how you speak. The emotions you convey need to be authentic and purposeful.

Oral stories should be relatively brief and simple, depending on the event. Novels provide plenty of time and space for character development and background information. A good oral storyteller develops the feelings of the character through paralanguage or the rate, pitch, and volume of your voice and through meaningful gestures and powerful words. The background can be laid out in efficiently with vivid language.

Memorable language

As you prepare for your storytelling presentation, consider metaphors and similes that would make your story more memorable. Write some of the sentences in your story and then change them to include a unique metaphor or simile. Or you could make your entire story metaphorical. In the book, *Tell to Win*, Peter Guber (2011, p. 149) proposes that metaphors and analogies provoke our imaginations. "The beauty of metaphors and analogies when used as story material is their economy. When they work, all the emotion and meaning you need can be delivered in a single image, sometimes a single word." The most provocative stories are often filled with figurative language.

I presented at a GED graduation to about sixty graduates and their families. I was asked to speak because I am a GED graduate, after dropping out of high school at the age of fifteen. The title of my presentation was "The Degree of a Second Chance." I told my audience how my diploma whispered to me that I had a second chance. At the age of thirty, I started college. By furthering my education, I was able to climb the rungs of fear, self-condemnation, ignorance, and dearth to step into the career of my dreams, and an increased self-esteem that I never thought possible. Education stops a cycle of ignorance and poverty, thrusting families into healthier and happier worlds. Even with metaphors, it is difficult to describe how different my frame of mind and heart has become through a college degree. Education changed the trajectory of my life and the lives of my children. Numerous audience members told me how much they appreciated and identified with my story. Hopefully, many of them went on to obtain a degree in higher education.

Be positive

Before you present, you need to be in a positive state of mind. Get rid of any negativity you are feeling and purposefully go before an audience prepared and ready to set the audience ablaze. Be energized and ready to tell your meaningful story in a compelling way. Every word, movement, and voice inflection should have a purpose.

There are speakers who are energized with negativity, but they move an audience by stirring hatred or fear. This kind of storytelling and this type of presentation are often poison. I hear people who make millions feeding off a frenzy of hatred. They have a faithful, core audience of people I would prefer to avoid, and they are building a reputation that will be frowned upon in years to come.

Visual aids

The most important visual aid in a story is your vivid words and body language. A few storytellers use PowerPoint presentations. There are great storytellers who effectively use props. My college has a Toastmasters Club, Toast to Education. One member brought in props in a speech to introduce herself.

She had various items that told us a little about her interests and priorities. She brought the props in a Christmas stocking because of her love for Christmas. She had refrigerator magnets because she had been given several by her friends and family as little gifts over the years. They speak of who she is—mother, wife, animal lover, friend, and traveler. Props are a creative way to bring a story to life.

Adapt

One of the great things about oral presentations is the ability to read an audience and adapt to the feedback that you are getting in this transactional environment. As you present, you may find times that the audience is really getting into a part of the story, and you can expound on that concept while giving another portion of the presentation less time than you had planned.

When Martin Luther King Jr. presented the most talked about speech in history, "I have a dream," he shifted from his notes to ad-libbing after one of King's friends called out to him, "Tell them about the dream, Martin. Tell them about the dream" (Bucktin, 2013). King chose to change the course of his presentation and ended up changing the course of history.

Body language

Your nonverbal communication is the key to being a successful storyteller. First, act confident no matter how you feel! Act like you are having fun or you are very passionate about the topic. If you mess up, do not stop, apologize, make annoying blah sounds, and so on. Do not memorize or read! Tell the story in your own way; it may be a little different every time you tell it. Look at your audience as your long lost friends. Smile and use effective silent pauses.

Be sure to set a rhythm and tempo of the presentation to match the mood you are setting. Increase volume to indicate action or excitement, and decrease volume to indicate sadness or suspense.

Activities

1. Choose one of the following stories and tell it without the use of notes. Concentrate on using vocal variety, gestures, facial expressions, and vivid language to tell the story.

   - Goldilocks and the Three Bears
   - The Ugly Duckling
   - The Hare and the Tortoise
   - Cinderella
   - The Three Little Pigs
   - Little Red Riding Hood
   - The Lion and the Mouse
   - The Boy Who Cried Wolf
   - Hansel and Gretel
   - Stone Soup

2. Choose one of the life events and tell it without the use of notes. Start with a hook. Concentrate on mood, vivid language, volume, and gestures.

   - Your scariest moment
   - The best moment of your life
   - An event that changed your life forever
   - Your most embarrassing experience
   - The day someone you love did something extraordinary
   - A time you stood up to a bully
   - A time when you lost
   - Your proudest moment
   - The day you met your partner
   - Explain the dumbest thing you or someone you know did

Story Preparation

In preparation for your story, give details about the following elements:

Setting (when and where)

Main character(s)

The mood of the story

The hook

The conflict

Unexpected ending

Story Evaluation Form

1. The story started with an interesting/entertaining hook._____

2. The main character(s) was developed._____

3. The plot of the story was developed._____

4. The story had compelling conflict._____

5. There was a clear climax._____

6. There was an unexpected twist to the story._____

7. Effective vocal variety and volume established the mood._____

8. Tempo and rhythm was demonstrated._____

9. The story was interesting and creative._____

10. The speaker used vivid words that added to the story._____

References

Bucktin, C. (2013) "Martin Luther King. The Story Behind the Famous 'I have a dream' speech that changed the course of America." *Mirror*. Retained from http://www.mirror.co.uk/news/world-news/martin-luther-king-story-behind-2178797#.UuVcFRAo5pg.

Gottschall, J. (2012) "Why Storytelling Is the Ultimate Weapon." *Co.Create*. Retrieved from http://www.fastcocreate.com/1680581/why-storytelling-is-the-ultimate-weapon

Guber, P. (2011) *Tell to Win*. New York: Random House.

McKee, R. and Fryer, B. (2014) "Storytelling That Moves People." *Harvard Business Review*. Retrieved from http://hbr.org/web/special-collections/insight/communication/storytelling-that-moves-people

Chapter Five

The Motivational Speech

The objectives of this chapter are to:

- ✓ Define motivational speeches.
- ✓ Brainstorm motivational speech topics.
- ✓ Explore a narrative motivational speech model.
- ✓ Apply a comparative advantages organizational style.
- ✓ Examine five parts of Monroe's Motivated Sequence.
- ✓ Explore techniques to enhance motivational speeches.

What Is a Motivational Speech?

The motivational speech is similar to a persuasive policy speech. Persuasion speeches are designed to convince others to change a value, attitude, or behavior. A topic of a persuasion speech that is not motivational could include topics of fact or value. For example, if I wanted to persuade my audience that the moon landing of 1969 was a hoax, that would be a question of fact. Was it a hoax or not? A value speech would be based upon questions of ethics. For instance, is it unethical to have a health-care plan that would provide funds for abortion? A motivational speech is more personal for the speaker and the audience. The motivational speech should induce or stir up emotion and inspire individuals to achieve something. In the end, a motivational speech will give the audience a strategy for success; however, the strategy or plan should be something simple. This emotional speech urges people to pursue a goal or correct a mistake while providing the formula for success.

The best motivational speakers relate to their audiences with compelling experiences. Speeches such as Martin Luther King Jr.'s "I Have a Dream" were birthed out of turmoil to motivate people to do the right thing. Similarly, Randy Pausch's "Last Lecture" reminds the audience that it is not the length of our lives but the quality of our lives that is important. Motivational speeches throughout history have moved people to action. Leaders, teachers, coaches, parents, and even movie speeches have impacted our lives.

Anyone who is going to lead others should learn to develop and present motivational speeches. Speeches that inspire others are given at sales meetings, graduations, business meetings, ceremonies, coaching sessions, receptions, seminars, and training sessions. This chapter will explain how to organize a motivational speech. The motivational speech is delivered with passion and is full of rich language. Use vivid personal examples that the audience can relate to. The motivational speech must also be well structured so the audience can follow along, and the call to action is doable, yet meaningful.

Motivational Topics

When choosing a topic, consider your own experiences. What personal growth lessons have you learned? Sometimes we can look back and discover some valuable changes that resulted from personal failures or hardships. You can even consider people who you admire and what you have learned from that individual that changed or molded your life. I gave a motivational speech about my grandmother who taught me to work hard, play hard, and help others every day. If you have a job where you give speeches to motivate employees, it is important that your audience feel that you are part of the team. They need to relate to you and be motivated by your life.

Below are famous motivational speech topics to guide you when considering a topic.

Speech Title	Speaker
"A Crisis of Confidence"	Jimmy Carter
"A Time for Choosing"	Ronald Reagan
"A Whisper of AIDS"	Mary Fisher
"Declaration of Conscience"	Margaret Chase Smith
"Fourteen Points"	Woodrow Wilson
"Give Me Liberty or Give Me Death"	Patrick Henry
"I Have a Dream"	Martin Luther King Jr.
"I've Been to the Mountaintop"	Martin Luther King Jr.
"I Really Hate My Job"	Zig Ziglar
"No Easy Walk to Freedom"	Nelson Mandela
"Now We Can Begin"	Crystal Eastman

"Plenty of Room at the Bottom"	Richard P. Feynman
"Responding to Landmines"	Princess Diana
"Setting Goals"	Zig Ziglar
"The Chance for Peace"	Dwight Eisenhower
"The Crisis"	Carrie Chapman Catt
"The Four Freedoms"	Franklin Delano Roosevelt
"The Last Lecture"	Randy Pausch
"The Perils of Indifference"	Eliezer Wiesel
"Truth and Tolerance in America"	Edward Kennedy
"We Shall Overcome"	Lyndon B. Johnson
"Wind of Change"	Harold Macmillan
"Women's Rights are Human Rights"	Hillary Rodham Clinton
"Yes We Can"	Barack Obama

Monroe's Motivated Sequence

In the 1930s, Alan Monroe created an organizational structure to assist in creating motivational speeches. This process has been used to motivate people to action in speeches and commercials. Monroe's Motivated Sequence comprises five parts of a motivational speech: Attention, need, satisfaction, visualization, call to action. These parts are to be used in order.

Attention

Begin your speech with an attention grabber. You must capture your audience's attention if you are going to hold their attention throughout the presentation. When you begin your speech, walk to the lectern, set any items you have down, take a breath and begin with your attention grabber. You do not tell people the topic of the speech or announce your name. A compelling motivational speech begins strong, with an attention grabber. Common attention grabbers that are effective include telling a dramatic story, arousing curiosity, startling your audience, telling the audience how the topic relates to their lives, asking a question, using a startling statistic, referring to a current event, or using humor.

If you are going to tell a *dramatic story*, make it as vivid as possible. People enjoy good stories. There are storytellers who are paid to tell dramatic stories. Do not read a story that you are telling your audience. Also, do not announce that you are going to tell a story. The audience will figure it out. It is also helpful if the story is about you or someone that you know. This provides you with credibility. When preparing your speech, think of a dramatic event that changed your life or the life of someone you know. A speaker who wanted to convince her audience to have regular mammograms told the audience a moving story about the day her mother found out that she had breast cancer. Her mother found a lump, but it was months before she went for testing. When she finally had a biopsy, it was too late. This story was a moving example to explain the need for women to take care of themselves for the sake of others.

Arousing curiosity draws in your audience, causing them to want to find out what you are speaking about. Use this method to lure your audience in, before you reveal your topic. A student, David Carroll, who was in one of my classes began his speech using this method. He brought a shoebox with the word *Monster* printed on it. A simple prop like this provides a sense of curiosity that is enjoyable and mysterious. Below is his introduction.

I.   There is a force that controls most every decision you will make, and it does so without you even noticing it is there.

   A. It tells you when to eat and when to work.
   B. It tells you when you should sleep and when you must get up.
   C. It never tires, it never rests. It is always present limiting your free time with its demands. (Attention Grabber is arousing curiosity)

II. In my research and throughout my life I have discovered that this force has the goal of completely controlling our lives, and for some it has succeeded. (Establish credibility with experience and research.)

III. Is this some form of conspiracy? Are there black helicopters circling overhead? No. We did this to ourselves. We created this monster. We set it in motion and have been bound by its hands ever since. Today, we will examine how this happened. How this force was created, and we will try to glimpse how much control it has on each one of us here today. (Preview)

IV. There is only one place to start, "What is this monster that controls us?"

(Transition: Opens the box and sets a clock on the table in front of him.)

Yes, the monster is a clock! If the speaker had said, "Hello, my name is David Carroll and I want to discuss how clocks control our lives," the speech would not have gathered the momentum that he provided. He lured us into the ideology of how an everyday device has power over us in such a way that made us want to listen.

The technique to *startle* your audience can also arouse curiosity. The idea is to do an action or say something that the audience would not expect. This does not mean that you bang on the lectern or scream. You do not want the audience to want or to run out of the room by the action; and never say something that would be offensive to your audience. If you use profanity, make an offensive comment, or insult people, you will not attract their attention but put up walls. Furthermore, do not try to shock the audience in a way that will turn people away by showing disgusting or unpleasant pictures. Although this may shock people, they are not going to want to listen if you turn their stomachs.

Use the startle-your-audience technique in such a way that it causes them to listen to you more closely because of the shock factor. I saw a person go to the lectern with a Coke can in his hand. He looked at everyone without uttering a word, drank the last swallow of Coke and threw the can in the corner. Then he said, "Is that okay?" The audience members were too dumbfounded to speak, so he repeated himself. "Is that okay?" About half of the audience responded, "No." Then he said, "Then why would we do this outside? Today, I want to talk to you about littering." Another speaker giving a speech about menopause came to the lectern with a battery operated fan. She was very dramatic as she went to the front of the classroom, blowing air on a few people along the way. It was a most enjoyable experience for the audience who wanted to hear what she had to say. In the end, startling your audience is not scaring or disgusting people. This is a method to perking people up in a way that will set them at the edge of their seats to listen.

Another attention-grabbing technique is to simply explain to the audience how the *topic relates to their lives.* When you are speaking, you are taking the valuable time of everyone in your audience. Let them know why it is important to their lives that they listen to you. People will be more attentive if they believe that what you are telling them will have a positive impact. Motivational speeches should be designed to help your audience. Explain the benefit at the very beginning. In other words, relate the topic to the needs of the audience. Imagine when you have paid close attention during a lecture in college. If the professor made a solid case about how the concept she was going to teach would help you, you tuned in longer. Sometimes instructors will mention that this information is on the test, and students who are not tuned in will focus at that moment, and maybe even jot down a note.

When you clearly *explain how a topic will be of value to your audience members,* they will be more focused on your speech. For example, if you were going to give a speech about overcoming nervousness during a presentation, you could begin by letting them know how your speech will assist them in the near future and throughout their lives. "Public speaking causes anxiety for most people in the world. Nonetheless, everyone in this room will be called upon to speak in front of others at some point. This may be in a classroom, at a ceremony, in a business meeting, at a wedding, or at a conference. If this thought makes you somewhat anxious or downright terrified, give me seven minutes of your time. I am going to discuss how to harness your public speaking fears so that you can speak with confidence."

Be specific when using this technique. Give the audience the reason they will need this information and when and where they can use it. For speeches less than fifteen minutes, giving the time frame can also be helpful. Telling my audience that I can teach them how to overcome an obstacle in their lives in seven minutes gives them a reason to give me seven minutes of their time. Be cautious that you do not exceed your time frame. If you suggest that you will talk for seven minutes, an alarm will sound in audience members' minds at seven minutes, and then you will lose them. If I think my speech will go eight minutes, I will tell them I am speaking for ten minutes. Then I speak for eight minutes. At a commencement address, a speaker stated that he would be speaking for fifteen minutes. At twelve minutes he said, "In conclusion," and I saw audience members sit up straight and move forward for the close. Then, after another fifteen minutes of him telling his life story, the audience members were not only zoned out and slumping in their chairs, but they disliked the man. He tricked us!

Asking a question can focus your audience on your topic. This is probably the easiest technique, so challenge yourself to use it only when it would be the most effective technique. Formulate a question that is simple to answer and will not embarrass your audience. It is also helpful to ask a question when combined with another attention grabber. For example, if you were going to present a speech about overcoming speech anxiety, like in the previous example, you could poll the audience. Only poll the audience if you believe that the majority will respond. When you ask the audience a question such as, "How many of you are at least a little anxious when you are called upon to speak in front of an audience?" raise your hand so they know that you are expecting a response. Then you can continue by relating the topic to the audience. "According to the *Book of Lists*, public speaking is the number one fear in the world. That means that most of you are nervous about speaking in public. This morning, I will give you some tips so that you can control your fear and become a more confident speaker." In doing this type of attention grabber, you have gotten your audience to participate and you have combined three attention grabbing techniques: asking a question, explaining the value of the topic to the audience, and using a startling statistic.

A startling statistic can be used by itself or with another technique. If you have a great statistic, back it up with a story. For example, "According to the National Highway Traffic Safety Administration, at this very moment, 660,000 drivers are talking on hand-held cell phones, and 1.18 million drivers are using some type of mobile device. Last year, six thousand people were killed because of distracted drivers and more than a half million were injured." This could be backed up by a story about someone who the speaker knows that was injured or killed by a person using a cell phone while driving. Statistics and a personal story drive the point home, adding the "this could be me" factor.

Statistics may be used in your attention grabber and also to support your speech. However, there are a few hints to follow whenever you include statistics in a speech. First, the statistic should be startling enough that we realize that it will affect someone we know. "According to the Domestic Violence Resource Center (2009), one in four women has experienced an assault by a husband or boyfriend. Do you know four women? In fact, six million women are victims of violence by a significant other each year." Secondly, if you use a statistic, tell the audience the source. This source must be credible to be effective. I would not state that "According to the democratic party Web site, the democrats will make great gains in the upcoming election." However, I could report that Gallup Poll has made such a claim.

Another thing to remember when using statistics is to round off large numbers. Your audience will not remember 9,932,811, so just say, "Almost ten million . . ." Also, do not stack more than three statistics at a time or you will lose the shock factor. If you give more statistics than that, you are really just rattling off a list of numbers and your audience will lose interest. Finally, be sure that your statistic is up-to-date. It would be of little effect to give a statistic about a social problem or technological advancement that is out-of-date. In summary, statistics can help provide your speech with credibility. If you tell your audience a credible source for the statistic, make sure that the statistic is powerful enough that the audience believes it could affect them or someone they know. Round off large numbers and only use one to three statistics in a row.

People want information that affects them now; therefore, *referring to a current event* can be helpful in gaining attention. This technique also relates the information to something they know. For example, if you want to draw attention to the social problem of child abuse, you could bring up a nationally publicized child abuse case. However, it is best to stay away from discussing a political party to a diverse audience. If you tell an audience that has differing viewpoints that you agree with a particular party, you will lose a portion of the audience right away. It is best to wait on discussing a controversial issue until you have gained their attention, established credibility, and related to the audience. Your attention grabber is to lure in the audience, not build walls.

Humor can draw an audience to the speaker, but use it with extreme caution. Humorous speeches are most memorable and enjoyable; however, humorous speeches can be difficult for people who are not naturally funny. I have heard speeches that started with a joke that did not relate to the topic and/or that did not get the audience laughter anticipated by the speaker. The attention grabber is to pull your audience into your topic. If you begin with a joke that does not focus on your topic, the purpose of the attention grabber is lost. Additionally, speakers who tell jokes that do not evoke laughter from the audience tend to get nervous. Then a brief silence will ensue and a sympathetic audience member will provide a fake laugh. This all works to erode the credibility of the speaker. When you choose to use humor, practice your speech in front of an honest audience and do not tell them the punch lines. If spontaneous laughter erupts, it is a go. In the event that you do incorporate humor in a speech and you do not get the desired response, move on. Do not use phrases like, "Tough crowd," or insult the audience with, "No sense of humor, huh." Also, do not try to explain the joke if they did not understand. Finally, do not make it a practice of insulting yourself to get a laugh, and certainly do not tell a joke that would insult a group such as an ethnic group.

If you want to start with humor, you may begin with a story that you have told before that consistently caused people to laugh. Those adept at storytelling may want to place humorous examples throughout the speech. It would not be wise to riddle your speech with amusing stories if it were a serious topic like AIDS. Nonetheless, a motivational speech could be structured like the entertaining after-dinner speech. After-dinner speeches should make a valuable point, but do so while making the audience laugh. For example, in my class lectures about conflict management, I tell stories about couples who use nonproductive conflict management styles like gunny sacking and steam rolling. We can all relate dramatic, amusing stories and assist in helping people remember the points.

Credibility

It is important that your audience understand why you are an expert on your topic. Introductions of keynote speakers should highlight the expertise of the speaker on the subject the speaker will be discussing, and should not be a lengthy biography of the speaker's life. A speaker who is not formally introduced must still provide credibility. This is simply done by letting the audience know that you are experienced in the topic or you have researched your topic. If your attention grabber is a story highlighting an experience you or a loved one has had, you have established yourself as an expert on the topic. For instance, when I gave a speech about the experiences I learned from my grandmother, I was sharing my experience. This provided me with credibility. If you have not had a personal experience with the topic that you shared in the attention grabber, tell your audience that you have researched the topic. "In my extensive research, I have discovered that laughter is a key element to our well-being."

Preview

Now that you have your audience's attention and have established yourself as the expert to discuss your topic, it is time to tell them what you are going to tell them. Make your preview a clear transition from your attention step to the body of your speech. "Today, I will explain why you need to have a positive attitude, three steps to achieving a positive attitude, and the benefits of a positive attitude in your career and in your personal life." This allows your audience to know exactly where you are taking them so they can easily follow along. It is redundant, but repetition assists the individuals in the audience to recall the information later.

Need

After you have gotten the attention of your audience, you establish a need or a problem that you are going to address. It is important that the individuals in the audience are convinced that it is a need that they have or that someone they care about has. You may start by stating the need and then back that up with stories, statistics, examples, and/or hypothetical situations. If you are giving a speech to a group of employees, it is good to use team members who you found demonstrating the positive characteristics you want as examples. Never call someone out in a bad way, but announcing successes is motivational.

It is important that your need step be compelling but organized. You may want to share a fact and then back this up with an example. Explain the disadvantages of the problem and the consequences during the need step. An example of this is provided at the end of this chapter in the outline speech "The Happiest Most Admired People on the Planet." Review the speech, "I Have a Dream" at the end of this chapter as well.

King provides fantastic imagery as he discusses the plight of African Americans and the need for equal rights for the good of all people.

In the end, establishing a need within our lives should be logically established so your audience will be compelled to change. A motivational speech is an important presentation that moves individuals to shift a paradigm for the good of an individual and eventually for the good of humankind.

Satisfaction

After your audience understands the need to change an attitude, belief, or behavior, give them a plan to do just that. The satisfaction step is a detailed plan to satisfy the need or solve a problem. The plan should also be something that the audience members can do. You ask for small things rather than expect the audience to change their lives. If you want your audience to exercise, ask them to start small or exercise twenty minutes, three times a week while doing an enjoyable activity.

The plan should explain the how, when, where, and why of the plan. If you are motivating a group to eat organic food, you should have already established the need for them to do this in the need step of the speech. In the satisfaction step, you explain how they can change to an organic diet gradually and as inexpensively as possible. Explain how one can substitute a different organic product each time they go to the grocery store. Organic foods are labeled, and grocery stores have sections designated for foods, free of dangerous chemicals. Health food stores are another alternative to a place to shop. Let your audience know that there is a health food store located near the mall at 439 Healthy Way. In this step, you do the research and make the transition as simple as possible for the audience.

In the speech example in this chapter "The Happiest Most Admired People on the Planet," I have asked the audience to change a behavior and an attitude. The information is broken down into two steps, be positive and be giving, but the plan is detailed. This is the longest part of the speech. Being happy and admirable is not a hard sell, but the how-to portion of the speech is detailed, simple, and easy to remember if change is to occur. Give a formula for success.

Visualization

The visualization step makes Monroe's Motivated Sequence unique to other persuasive speech organizational patterns such as problem/solution, problem/cause/solution, cause and effect, or advantages/disadvantages. In this step, you give your audience a view of their world if they will follow your plan. You may also explain to them how their lives will be if they do not do what you asked. When considering this step, let your audience hear, smell, taste, see, and touch the world with and without the change. You will want to consider what types of verbs you are using. Use active, descriptive verbs. Consider using figurative language such as metaphors and similes to draw a more vivid image of your idea. There is an example of this in the speech at the end of the chapter. "The Happiest Most Admired People on the Planet" uses the visualization step. "I Have a Dream" is full of vivid visualization. King painted a picture of the world that he dreamed of, which made this the most memorable speech of this century.

Call to Action

The final step in Monroe's Motivated Sequence is to call the audience to take action. You have given them a plan to satisfy the need in the satisfaction step, but this is a final call to seal the deal. This needs to be very specific to individuals and something that is basic. If you have laid out a plan to eat organic food, you may now want to request that the next time individuals are in the grocery store and reach for an apple, pick up an organic apple. If you are encouraging your audience to exercise and have given them a detailed plan in the satisfaction step, you may want them to get up twenty minutes earlier in the morning and take a brisk walk or take the stairs this week rather than the elevator.

As you move to your call to action, give some type of signal that you are coming to a close. This could be "In conclusion" or "Let me conclude with" or "What did I learn from this" or "In summary" etc. However, when you have signaled, do not trick the audience and add new information or make this point seven of your speech. The conclusion of the speech is like taking the main points, wrapping them up, and giving your audience the central idea so they can take the overall point of your speech home. The last part is a final push or call to action.

Tell them something specific that they can do to move them toward the attitude, belief, or action that you are persuading them to do.

The conclusion of your speech should be the most memorable. When you signal the conclusion, you tune the audience into your speech. People's minds wander, even in a seven-minute speech. We have been trained to listen in when someone signals the end. Just watch them the next time you give a speech and say, "In conclusion." You can almost hear the wave of voices saying, "Listen up. She/he is almost finished! It is time to get our package of what we are to remember from this speech now." Then very briefly give them their summary package and the little step toward change.

Then it is time for you to be quiet. It is a temptation to continue talking after your conclusion. When I taught elementary school, my students would write "The End" at the end of their stories or essays. I would cross this out and ask that they not do that in the future. I had a fourth-grade student ask how I would know that the story had ended if he did not write "The End" at the end. I told him that there were no more words to read, so I could figure it out. It is the same when presenting a speech. When the last powerful word has come out of your mouth and you are silent, your audience will know that you are finished.

If you think you must say something at the end, make it "Thank you" or "Thank you for listening." It is so tempting at the end of a speech to say something to weaken the speech such as, "Well, that's all I got." If you signaled your conclusion, provided a summary, and gave a simple thing to do, you have powerfully concluded. If you stop talking, people will know that you are finished and clap.

Comparative Benefits

Another organizational pattern for motivational speeches is comparative benefits pattern. This pattern follows the same guidelines as Monroe's Motivated Sequence in that you gain the attention of the audience, establish your credibility, and give a preview of your presentation. Then you will show a need. In the satisfaction step, you will compare two or more solutions and explain why one solution is best. This has been effectively used in business presentations.

Comparative advantages or comparative benefits can be used to compare and contrast two or more items, solutions to problems, choices, or brands. The goal is simple, show why one thing is more beneficial than something else. Visualization is used within the comparison stage while explaining the advantages. This speech should motivate others that a change will bring value to their lives as opposed to the status quo.

Narrative Speeches

Another way to present a motivational speech is through storytelling. In first-person narratives, the speaker is telling a personal experience. One can also tell stories about the lives of others. Storytelling is discussed in detail in Chapter 4 of this text. To motivate an audience to act, the audience must have an emotional investment in the topic. Stories that are rich with figurative language, vocal variety, and effective gestures can stir emotion in an audience.

Make it Personal

Toastmasters International (2008) suggests that effective motivational speeches are riddled with quotes and personal stories. If you share a story or have a personal experience about your topic, this will cause you to be most enthusiastic and will provide you with a level of expertise. You may begin your first story in your attention grabber. This provides you with credibility and allows the audience to begin identifying with you early. Consider using humorous, personal stories. Do not criticize yourself in these stories because this makes the audience uncomfortable; however, funny stories where you laugh at yourself or circumstances make a speech enjoyable to listen to.

It is not necessary that your personal stories be humorous to be effective. I have heard powerful stories and examples that evoked emotions such as sadness and anger. There are personal stories that can cause the audience to become fearful, but fear appeals only work under certain conditions that will be considered later in the chapter. Giving the right amount of personal information is effective, but giving too much personal information can turn your audience away. Do not discuss information that would be deemed inappropriate. Also, do not use language that might be offensive to some audience members. You want your audience to hang on your every word and not cringe at certain words.

The Principle Must Be Applicable and Simple

"People aren't motivated by what you say; they're motivated by what they understand" (Toastmasters International, 2008, par. 7). The purpose of any speech is not to convince your audience that you are a genius. The focus should be on the principle that you are relaying and your audience. People are egocentric by nature. They are interested in and relate all information to themselves. If you make the information too difficult for them to understand, they will not listen or like you. Additionally, if you talk down to them, it will appear that you are trying to make them feel ignorant. Keep it simple, but not in a condescending way.

To persuade someone to change an attitude, belief, or behavior, the concept must be practical. The speech needs to be well structured and the language clear.

Figurative Language

When you are creating your motivational speech masterpiece, season it with figurative language. Powerful language yields powerful speeches. These phrases include metaphors, similes, alliterations, repetitions, antitheses, personifications, and analogies. Metaphors make unique comparisons. Similes make unique comparisons using like or as. Repetition is when you use a word or phrase over and over to lend cadence to the speech. Antithesis sets two contrasting ideas together. Personification gives human traits to a non-living object. Analogies transfer ideas from one subject to another.

Below are examples of each.

FIGURATIVE LANGUAGE	EXAMPLE	SPEECH TITLE	SPEAKER
Metaphor	*Brick walls are there for a reason. The brick walls are not there to keep us out. The brick walls are there to show how badly we want something. Because the brick walls are there to stop the people who don't want something badly enough.*	The Last Lecture	Randy Pausch
Simile	*Dangers and difficulties have not deterred us in the past; they will not frighten us now. But we must be prepared for them like men in business who do not waste energy in vain talk and idle action.*	"No Easy Walk to Freedom"	Nelson Mandela
Repetition	*Let freedom ring.*	"I Have a Dream"	Martin Luther King Jr.
Antithesis	*Your success as a family… our success as a society depends not on what happens in the White House, but on what happens inside your house.*	"Wellesley College Commencement"	Barbara Bush
Personification	*Because HIV asks only one thing of those it attacks: Are you human?*	"A Whisper of AIDS"	Mary Fisher
Analogy	*We must especially beware of that small group of selfish men who would clip the wings of the American eagle in order to feather their own nests.*	Four Freedoms	Franklin D. Roosevelt

Emotional Appeals

A gifted speaker can persuade others that a principle or idea is correct by showing evidence that backs up a point. In other words, I will agree or disagree with a conjecture if I can see that the argument is sound, and I find you to be a credible person. However, a person is more prone to be motivated to action if the individual has an emotional investment. Emotions move people to do something. Emotional appeals that are not backed with logic and principled motives by the speaker are unethical. Unfortunately, emotion appeals have been used to manipulate audiences to make poor choices, such as to do something violent.

When you are developing a persuasive speech, provide your audience with logical evidence and establish your credibility by telling about your research and/or your experience with the topic. Also consider what emotions your topic should stir up in you and your audience. Common emotions include pride, hope, sadness, guilt, anger, disgust, fear, interest, surprise, and happiness. Fear is a short-lived emotion and is effective if the audience feels vulnerable, and you have provided a real way of relieving the fear. People who have smoked for many years and do not feel that they can stop smoking will brush aside fear appeals by bringing up someone they knew who smoked many years and did not die of lung cancer.

It is easier to focus on a speech that stirs up positive emotions. For instance, stimulating hope to encourage me to vote would be more motivational than using fear. Fear may work to encourage me to vote one time, but hope or pride may be more useful in motivating me to vote for years to come. As you consider your speech topic, choose the emotions that you want your audience to experience. Hopefully, most of the experiences that you provide will be positive.

Quotes

Quotes are powerful tools to use to begin your speech, end your speech, or support a point within your speech. Use quotes sparingly, but a powerful quote can drive home a point. With the use of the Internet, quotes are easy to find. You can use a search engine and simply type the topic and quotes and you will discover that someone has said something clever about your topic. You can even find quotes about quotes like this one from an unknown author: "You have the right to remain silent. Anything you say will be misquoted, then used against you." A quote that is more than two lines is not quotable or memorable. The best quotes in speeches are unique, short, and witty and relate directly to the topic. You may also find proverbs that are meaningful in motivational speeches. I can still remember two African Proverbs that I heard in a speech more than twenty years ago: 1. Don't tell the man who is carrying you that he stinks. 2. Live chicks do not do well under a dead hen. Remember to use quotes and proverbs sparingly so they are memorable. Say a quote or proverb slowly and pause for a moment to allow it to anchor in the minds of your audience. It is also effective to use a powerful quote or proverb as your final words.

When telling the quote, be sure to let the audience know who said the quote. If I wanted to use a favorite quote, I would say, "Tom Stoppard said, 'Words are sacred. They deserve respect. If you get the right ones in the right order, you can nudge the world a little.'" A quote said with conviction is a potent instrument for the motivational speaker.

Summary

Motivational speeches are presentations that inspire an audience to change a belief, attitude, or behavior. The topic of the motivational speech should be meaningful to the speaker. The speaker should have personal experience with the topic and a passion to move others. One organizational style to develop a motivational speech is Monroe's Motivated Sequence. This structure breaks the motivational speech into five sections: attention, need, satisfaction, visualization, and action. Comparative benefits and narrative speeches are also effective organizational patterns for the motivational speech. The content of the speech should include personal examples and be understandable to the audience without being condescending. Use powerful language and provide the audience with an emotional experience. Quotes can be used for a dramatic, memorable outcome.

Discussion Questions

1. What is your favorite movie motivational speech? What made the speech memorable?
2. Read the motivational speech outline "The Happiest Most Admired People on the Planet" at the end of this chapter. Looking back on the list of emotions in the chapter, which emotions does the speech evoke and why?

The Happiest Most Admired People on the Planet

Specific purpose: To persuade my audience that being positive and giving leads to happiness.

Central Idea: There are two keys to living a happy life that others want to follow. These keys are to be positive and to be giving.

Attention

I.   Who is the one person that you admire the most? The person I admired the most was my grandmother. I would guess that she has some of the same characteristics that the person you are thinking of has. She was caring, giving, positive, and enjoyable to be around. I would even say that she was happy.

II. Would you like to be that kind of person, the kind of person that others admire and strive to be like? According to my extensive research and personal experiences, there are some simple things that you can do that will make you an admirable person.

III. Over the next eight minutes, I will give you two keys to living a happier life that others will want to emulate.

Need

I.   One of our constitutional rights is the pursuit of happiness. However, according to a 2009 Gallup Poll, about one half of Americans suggest they experience "a lot of happiness/ enjoyment without a lot of stress" (Gallup, 2009). A study by the University of Pennsylvania (Nauert, 2009) suggests that the number of people in the United States reported happiness has not changed much over the past thirty years. Although the percentage of people who reported being "pretty happy" increased from 49 percent in 1972 to 56 percent in 2006, those who claimed to be "very happy" decreased.

II. Aristotle said, "Happiness depends on ourselves." Researchers suggest that increasing your happiness is up to you (Ephraim, 2009).

III. In the book, *How We Chose to Be Happy*, Rick Foster and Greg Hicks (2000) suggest that happiness is a choice. Those most admired are those who make that choice to be happy.

IV. Now that we know that we can choose to be happy and respected, how do we pursue this dream?

Satisfaction

I. There are many books, articles, and prescriptions to becoming happy and respected. Of the ones that I have read, it all comes down to two keys or should I say two bes: be positive and be giving.

A. You should wake up every morning and declare that you will have a positive attitude.

1. Being positive starts with being positive with you. Be determined to tell yourself nice things about you and those around you. You cannot be a positive, optimistic person unless you are kind to yourself.

2. Be positive with those around you. Do not speak negatively to others. Remember, their happiness depends upon a healthy self-esteem. Try to help others to increase their self-esteem.

a) Every day, do at least one thing that will increase someone else's self-esteem. This may be writing a server's manager a note about the good service you received or sincerely giving someone a specific compliment. "I appreciate the way that you are so willing to help others, such as when you have the coffee brewing for everyone in the office every morning."

b) Smile and say positive things to those you meet. When asked how you are, tell people something positive. I knew a young woman who talked about how sick or sad she was every time someone asked, "How are you?" It made those around her stop asking.

3. Consider the positive things that happen to you every day and ponder on these things rather than the negative.

    a) Negativity is a spiral. Once your mind starts to dwell on the negative, it will spiral down.
    b) I have a good friend who I admire. Every time I see him, he starts the conversation about something uplifting. No matter how it looks outside, it is a beautiful day. I want to be like that.

B. Secondly, be giving.

    1. When you are positive, you are giving others a more positive outlook on life. But don't stop there.
    2. If giving to others does not come naturally to you, then plan to do something kind for at least one person every day.

        a) You may help someone with a project, buy muffins for the people in your office, walk a dog at an animal shelter, or take the trash can to the curb for an elderly neighbor.
        b) There are books and articles you may read that will give you ideas about doing small acts of kindness.

II. My grandmother worked long hours everyday. She owned a nursing home and prepared delicious meals for her patients. She prepared a plate for each patient, and consistently made dishes that were her patients' favorites.

A. I remember her positive attitude with others and about life in general. She laughed out loud every day, and this laughter was infectious.
B. She did acts of kindness for others every day. She often took nursing home patients home with her. She would take them shopping and out to eat. She always went to work with a few candy bars in her purse to give away.
C. I loved going to her house in the summers. I went with her to work and enjoyed visiting with the patients, who

I considered my friends. It did not feel like I was giving to them, but their eagerness to talk to me boosted my self-esteem.

Visualization

I. Imagine the world with people who are happy because they have chosen to be positive and giving. If you consistently think about the positives in your life, you will begin to see more and more positives in your life. Focus in on the good things and brush off the little negative barbs that could steal your happiness. Especially do not allow negative, hateful people to rob you of any moments of happiness. And your positive attitude will be a beacon that draws others to you.

II. If you consistently mull over the negative things in your life and about other people, you will be drawn down into a dungeon of despair. In that dark place, others will withdraw or they will be overtaken by your shadows. When life does become gloomy, seek out those who are positive. They will help lift you up. Afterward, you can move forward and assist others out of their dark places.

Call to Action

I. In conclusion, we admire those who are positive and those who are giving.

II. Those who are caring, giving, and positive are also the happiest people on the planet.

III. If you want to not only pursue happiness but obtain it, then you must be positive with yourself and with others. Determine to think and say positive things about yourself, your friends, and your life. And every day, go out of your way and do at least one simple act of kindness every day.

IV. Happiness can be summed up by the words of Helen Keller: "Happiness cannot come from without. It must come from within. It is not what we see and touch or that which others do for us which makes us happy; it is that which we think and feel and do, first for the other fellow and then for ourselves."

V.   When you wake up tomorrow, share a little act of kindness to one other person. Share a specific compliment to your server or the person that you are face-to-face with. I challenge you to make the day of one person every day.

VI. Start right now. Say out loud to yourself: "I wish you all of the happiness in the world." Now everyone, look at a person next to you and repeat after me, "I wish you all of the happiness in the world."

References

Ephraim, N. (2009, Nov. 8). The pursuit of happiness becomes true happiness. Selfhelp Magazine. Retrieved from *http://www.selfhelpmagazine.com/article/the-pursuit-of-happiness*

Foster, R. and Hicks, G. (2000). *How We Chose to Be Happy*. Perigee Trade.

Gallup. (2009, Dec. 21). Gallup Daily: U.S. Mood. Retrieved from *http:// www.gallup.com/poll/106915/Gallup-Daily-US-Mood.aspx*

Nauert, R. (2009, Feb. 26). Happiness in America. *PsychCentral*. Retrieved from *http://psychcentral.com/news/2009/01/27/happiness-in- america/3706.html*

Motivated Sequence Outline Template

Title _____

Attention Step: (tell a dramatic story, arouse curiosity, startle your audience, tell the audience how the topic relates to their lives, ask a question, use a startling statistic, refer to a current event, or use humor).

_____
_____
_____
_____
_____
_____

Establish Credibility—Explain why you are qualified to discuss the topic.

_____
_____

Preview Speech: Today, I will explain _____
_____
_____
_____
_____

Need Step: Establish a need using logical proof and emotional proof.

Satisfaction Step: Explain how the need can be satisfied. Provide a plan.

Visualization Step: Paint a picture of what the world looks like if the need is and/or is not satisfied.

Action Step: Summarize your speech and then give your audience a *specific* call to action. What do you want them to do or how do you want them to think differently?

In Conclusion,

References

Domestic Violence Resource Center. (2009). *Domestic violence statistics.* Retrieved   from   http://www.dvrc-or.org/domestic/violence/ resources/ C61/.

Lupus Foundation of America. (2009). *LFA committed to bringing down the barriers to finding new treatments for people with lupus.* Retrieved from http://www.lupus.org/webmodules/webarticlesnet/ templates/ new_researchlfa.aspx?articleid=142&zoneid=31.

National Highway Traffic Safety Administration. (2014, Feb.). *Traffic Safety Facts. National Center for Statistics and Analysis.* Retrieved from http://www-nrd.nhtsa.dot.gov/Pubs/811884.pdf.

Transcript: Barack Obama's Speech on Race. "A More Perfect Union." Retrievedfromhttp://www.npr.org/templates/story/story.php?story Id=88478467.

Self Improvement Mentor.com. (2009). *List of human emotions we can experience.* Retrieved from http://www.self-improvement-mentor. com/ list-of-human-emotions.html

Speech Guru. (2008). *Motivational Speech.* Retrieved from http:// www. speech-guru.com/motivational_speech.php.

Toastmasters International. (2008). *Motivational speech techniques.* Retrieved from http://www.toastmasters.org/MainMenuCategories / Free Resources/Questions about Leadership/Conflict Resolution/ MotivationalSpeechTechniques.aspx.

United States Department of Transportation. (2009). *New research finds increase in use of hand-held devices among all drivers.* Retrieved from http://www.nhtsa.dot.gov/

Chapter Six

Interviews

The objectives of this chapter are to:

- ✓ Understand the need for interviewing strategies.
- ✓ Obtain experience in my field of study.
- ✓ Sell yourself.
- ✓ Plan to make a good first impression.
- ✓ Incorporate nonverbal language.
- ✓ Responses to interview questions.
- ✓ Construct a follow-up letter.
- ✓ Perform phone interviews.
- ✓ Productively turn people down.

I have taught college for more than eleven years. Few of the students who have attended college are there simply for personal growth. The vast majority attend college in pursuit of the job of their dreams. Although personal growth is a by-product of education, it is not the goal of incoming freshmen. A degree is not the only need in landing the job of your dreams. One must also be able to design a fantastic resume that shows experience and essential skills. Knowing how to search for a job, constructing a cover letter, acing the interview, and writing a follow-up thank-you letter is important to learn, in order to obtain a dream job. Interviewing skills are also needed when enrolling in a graduate school or pursuing a scholarship. Managers or people who will interview others should also be equipped in conducting interviews that help companies or organizations select the right people.

The Significance of Interview Strategies

I was speaking with a student who was a computer genius. He told me that he had the skills for a good job, but he did not do well during interviews. In his pursuit for a job, he would get to the interview with a polished resume, experience, and expertise, but he would lose the job during the interview. You can obtain the career of your dreams if you will obtain your degree, gain experience by volunteer work and internships, develop an impressive cover letter, resume, and follow-up letter, and implement effective interview strategies. Job searches are not for the halfhearted or fainthearted. It is a full-time job that takes determination and confidence. Be prepared to put many hours into the pursuit. Read books and articles about job hunting. One well-known book is *What Color Is Your Parachute? A Practical Manual for Job-hunters and Career-changers* by Richard Bolles. The author updates the book every year, so it would be best to get the newest edition. There are books and articles with common interview questions and ways to answer these questions. If you conduct job interviews, these books are a good resource as well. There are also books that give detailed instruction on how to conduct the interview. Effective interviews are essential in assisting employers find the person best suited for the job.

Preparing for the Interview

It is important to prepare for the interview before you begin applying for jobs. Interview others who are in career fields of interest. This is a good way to get to know people in the field, and it will give you valuable information for your job interview. It would be even better if you shadowed a few people or followed them around for a day. Ask people who are working in your field of interest the following questions and think of other questions.

- o Explain a typical work day.
- o What skills are needed for your job?
- o What are the qualities or traits needed to be great in this career?
- o Do you know any companies or organizations hiring people in this field?
- o What is your favorite part of this job?
- o What is your least favorite part of this job?
- o What advice could you give someone pursuing this career?

College students should do this type of interview in their last year or two of school. Joining clubs and professional organizations assist in networking as well. It is not luck or stumbling into the right place at the right time. Those who are in the right place at the right time to obtain jobs are the ones who are going to the right places and meeting the right people. You are not going to meet the right people if you do not put forth the effort.

Getting Experience

If you want to work for a particular company or organization, do volunteer work or work as an intern for that institution. You need to show experience on your application. Internships allow you to gain experience in your field. Be sure that you wow the people you work with when you are doing your internship. The internship should be considered a daily interview. Always be positive, show up early, and do your very best work. Do some type of volunteer work in your field. If you cannot find a volunteer job that aligns with the type of job that you would like to do, then volunteer anyway. Volunteerism will help immensely when applying for scholarships and it helps you network with others in the community. Even if you can only volunteer one hour a week, it would be helpful. If you are going into education, volunteer at a school. If you are going into construction or engineering, volunteer at Habitat for Humanity or with community cleanup programs. Accountant majors could offer free bookkeeping services at a nonprofit organization. People going into the medical profession could volunteer at hospitals or health clinics. You might also contact your local United Way to discover additional organizations that need your help or look up a list of nonprofit organizations on the Internet.

Research

You will write a cover letter and adapt your resume or curriculum vitae to the company with which you are applying. Before you do this, begin your research. You should look up the vision and mission statements of the company, and you can mention this in the cover letter. Look up the job description on the company Web site and adapt your resume and cover letter accordingly. If the job you are applying for was in an ad, then use the wording from the ad to explain how you have the qualifications for the job and the skills that they are looking for.

Before the interview, thoroughly research the company. Learn as much as you can about the history, salaries, work environment, and job duties. Write down how your skills match the job duties. Also consider your personality traits that would make you a good fit for the job. Examples of these traits include:

Energetic	Friendly	Positive	Sincere
Loyal	Ambitious	Enthusiastic	Sociable
Decisive	Devoted	Cheerful	Sympathetic
Considerate	Kind	Determined	Caring
Flexible	Focused	Hardworking	Calm
Optimistic	Cooperative	Honest	Alert
Confident	Self-directed	Respectful	Detail oriented
Disciplined	Motivated	Reliable	Conscientious
Lifelong learner	Imaginative	Graceful	Visionary
Objective	Open-minded	Patient	Resourceful
Supportive	Intuitive	Good listener	Risk taker
Leadership	Communicator	Speaking skills	Teamwork
Problem solver	Flexible	Planner	Punctual
Empathic	Persistence	Systematic	Consistent
Responsible	Immediate	Intelligent	Helpful
Attentive	Levelheaded	Polite	Even-tempered
Creative	Trustworthy	Fast learner	Understanding

Selling Yourself

During the interview, you are selling yourself. You need to explain how you are the best match for the job. At the beginning of the interview, listen to the interviewers. Let them explain the job, the duties, and the interview process. Use immediacy behaviors, be positive, and act confident but not aloof. Imagine yourself being the interviewer. How should someone behave if you were considering him or her for a job in your organization? As you answer your questions, explain how your traits are the traits needed for the job. Give specific examples about how you were creative, energetic, or patient.

If you are interviewing for a teaching job, you would consider characteristics of excellent teachers including patience, caring, organization skills, and lifelong learning. Think of examples where you have displayed these characteristics in your work or volunteer experiences.

Have clear examples about how you have experience and expertise to carry out the duties of the job. You should also understand the company environment and know that you are a good fit. I was working with a search committee, and we were interviewing people for a community college assistant professor position. The man we were interviewing had the education and experience, but he did not understand the community college environment. We are student focused, and when he referred to community college students as "those students" and "students who could not begin at the university level," we were not impressed. Our students choose to start at a community college because of various reasons. It is a great place to begin their college experience. The people on that committee and the faculty and staff at my college respect our students, many of whom are working, raising families, and going to school full time. This individual used wording that made it clear that he was not a good fit to teach at a community college. Know the priorities of the company or organization. You should also consider if you would feel comfortable in the environment as well.

Introducing Yourself

The first few minutes of the interview is the most crucial. You will have bathed, cleaned your nails, washed and combed your hair, and brushed your teeth. Go easy on cologne or perfume. If you are interviewing for a professional job, wear a professional, well-fitted suit that is black, pin-striped, or navy. Shoes are professional, closed-toe, clean, and should match your belt.

Arrive fifteen minutes early. Take a few minutes to look at yourself in a mirror and make sure that your clothes and makeup have not faltered on your way there. You should have a professional-looking Padfolio with a copy of your resume, cover letter, pad and pen, and examples of your work. Always be friendly and respectful. Let the receptionist know that you have arrived and sit down. Act as though everyone you meet may have input about you getting the job. Do not pace in the lobby or waiting area. Be patient and as relaxed as possible.

When someone calls your name, stand, smile, walk over, shake hands, and introduce yourself: "Good morning. My name is Ruth Livingston, and I am so happy to be here." The handshake is important to an interview so practice with someone who will tell you if your handshake is too hard or soft. If a committee is interviewing you, shake the hands of those conducting the interview. If you have not been told, ask where they would like for you to sit. Then, sit down, take out your notepad, and write the names of each person so you can send them a thank-you card or letter after the interview. You may also ask for the business cards of the interview to get names, titles, and e-mail addresses.

Appear as relaxed as possible, and allow them to do most of the talking during this important phase. Never, ever interrupt. You are to be friendly, likeable, and professional. Being loud, boisterous, timid, or arrogant does not make a positive first impression. When you practice interviewing with friends or family, go through the introduction stage and get their opinions. Practice enough times that it does not feel awkward. Typically, first impressions are forever.

If you are the interviewer, consider the intimidating atmosphere that you may create and try to make the interviewee as relaxed as possible. Introduce yourself with a smile. Tell the interviewee that you appreciate his or her time and interest. The interview should be conducted in a comfortable area. Let the interviewee know where to sit, and offer something to drink. If there is a committee, make the introductions. You will find out more about a person who feels comfortable enough to talk with you and your committee. An aloof, intimidating demeanor will not attract the most skilled employees to your workforce. The interviewer(s) will be making a first impression as well. If you want to attract and retain the best, treat them with respect.

Nonverbal Language

Researchers suggest that we convey 65 to 93 percent of face-to-face communication through nonverbal messages (Beebe, Beebe & Ivy, 2006). We tend to believe nonverbal messages over the verbal messages. For example, if I say that I am happy to be here and I am slumped over as if I am sad, you will believe that I am not happy to be here. You should use nonverbal language that conveys what you are saying. Also, be very attentive. Make eye contact that is natural to everyday conversation when you are talking with a group of people about a topic that really interests you. Do not stare anyone down. When asked a question, smile, look at the person asking the question, and then answer the question making eye contact conversationally with all of the interviewers. Lean forward, and sit poised but not rigid. Do not fidget with your papers, pen, hair, jewelry, or pick lint off your clothes. These are nervous habits that are distracting. If you are nervous, keep it to yourself. It is an uncomfortable situation, and most people interviewing for the job of their dreams will be nervous.

Write down any information that you will want to refer to later, but do not write the questions. Hands should be placed in front of you on the table or in your lap. Watch lip licking, and do not have gum, candy, or food in your mouth. Also, do not bring a cell phone in with you. Leave it in the car. You may forget to turn it off. Nothing says incompetence like a cell phone ringing or vibrating during an interview. Use a friendly, conversational tone throughout.

Your rate, pitch, and volume should be comfortable for everyone. Also, eliminate tag questions, vocalized pauses, and self-criticism from your language in every occasion (Devito, 2006). Tag questions are when you are making a statement, but you raise the pitch in your voice so it sounds like a question. Or you add a word like, "Okay?" after your statements. This weakens your message and makes you sound uncertain. When you go for an interview, interviewers usually do not let you know if they like your answers, but you would really like a response. You are asked to list your three greatest strengths. You answer in the form of a question because you would like a response, "I am loyal, energetic, and optimistic??" This makes you appear wishy-washy and unsure about your strengths. Instead, confidently answer, "I am loyal to a company that has given me the opportunity to work. I am energetic in providing a focused effort to a job that I care about. And I am optimistic because a positive attitude is essential to personal and professional growth."

Vocalized pauses should also be omitted from your communication events. When you want to "um," "and ah," or "like," substitute with a moment's pause. If you get tongue-tied, do not make some strange noise to compensate. Take a second to breathe, and then start again. Finally, do not say anything bad about yourself or anyone you have ever known in your entire life. Be positive. We self-criticize when we are searching for compliments. It makes you appear unsure of yourself.

Immediacy behaviors that are addressed in a previous chapter are effective nonverbal communication tools. Think about the people who you enjoy working with. They are friendly, honest, kind, and pay compliments. Display these behaviors in the interview and every day at work. If you are having personal problems or are in a bad mood, do not let it show. Use open posture, active listening, and vocal variety to demonstrate your communication skills.

STAR Interviews

One suggestion for giving good interviews is the STAR method. STAR stands for Situation, Task, Activity, and Result. First, describe the situation and the task that needed to be accomplished. Use specific examples rather than a generalization. The situation and task should be relevant to a professional situation. Then explain the action that you took. Again be specific telling what you actually did. Finally, explain the results. You will also explain what you accomplished and what you learned from the situation (Higgins, 2013).

Responses That Achieve Results

It is important that you are prepared for any questions that you will be asked. There are lists of typical questions asked in books and on Internet sites. Be prepared for the top questions asked, and follow-ups to the questions. Listen to the complete question. If you need to clarify or think that you do not understand all or part of the question, rephrase the question, or ask the person to repeat the question. Look at the person asking the question, but make eye contact with the group when answering.

Paul Michael (2005) wrote an article about the twenty-three most asked interview questions and a strategy to develop answers. A more comprehensive list of questions are in the book, *Monster Careers: Interviewing* (2005) and in Richard Beatty's book, *The Interview Kit* 3rd ed. (2003). Read the information in these and other books when you are applying for a job. Answer the questions and give brief examples. Do not discuss examples that are personal. You should give professional examples. Below are 12 frequently asked interview questions.

1. *Tell us a little about yourself.*
   This is not a request to give a biography. You could mention your love for the career or why you went into this profession. You may want to mention some of your greatest professional

accomplishments, professional goals, and present situation. Do not tell them about your children and what they are doing in school, or discuss your parents. You are selling yourself and your professional expertise.

2. *Tell us about the professional experience that you have as a* _____ *(insert job).*

   If you have experience in the field, go through the list. If you are just coming out of college, you should carefully consider how you will answer this question. You may mention the volunteer work and internship where you have worked in the field. If you developed a portfolio in college, now is the time to show your work. Explain why you are in this field of study. You may have worked with people in customer service or as a server while you were going to college. Link these experiences with the duties of the job for which you are interviewing. Do not drone on and on about experiences that you have had that do not apply. Be positive about your past work experiences. If you did not enjoy your previous job, keep it to yourself. Just highlight your professional or collegiate experiences as it relates to this particular position.

3. *What are your three greatest strengths or what would you suggest is your greatest strength?*

   This opens the door for you to pitch your positive qualities. Think of three in order of importance if you are only asked your one greatest strength. Tell the strength and then give an example about how you manifest this positive quality. For example: "My greatest strength would be my sense of loyalty. I believe that a company that gives me the opportunity to work, deserves my full attention and hard work. Loyalty also includes building the company and my colleagues up rather than being critical. At my last job, I volunteered to take on challenges above my regular job description. One example is when I worked after-hours to design a new training module for incoming servers. It was an exciting challenge where I could use my expertise to make positive changes for my employer." Think of the strengths that you have that would be an asset to this organization. It should always be positive and related to the position. Being a good mom is a positive strength, but only describe professional qualities, not personal qualities.

4. *What is your biggest weakness?*

This is perhaps the most dreaded question, but it is frequently asked. The interviewer wants to know that you can point out your weaknesses and that you can develop a strategy to work on them. Do not be too honest and say something like, "I do not like working with women." or too personal, "I drink too much." or try to make a strength a flaw, "I have been told that I work too hard." Bring up a minor flaw and explain your strategy for improvement.

The flaw that you choose should not be a key need to the position that you seek. A nurse applying for a job in the Emergency Room should not tell the interviewer that he does not work well under pressure. When I applied for my present position, I was asked about my greatest weakness. I told the interview committee, "I am concerned that I may grade student speeches too leniently, and that I will not be consistent. To remedy this, I am working to improve my speech evaluation rubric. This has helped me to more fairly assess speeches but gives me data concerning specific areas that I need to focus on when teaching." Let the interviewer know that you can recognize your own weaknesses and find ways to improve.

5. *Describe a professional or academic failure you have had and how you recovered from it*

This is similar to the previous question. This question is designed to get you to thinking about your failures. Failure is not a negative as everyone fails at some time or another. As Zig Ziglar points out "Failure is an event, not a person." It's how you respond to that failure that is what the interviewer is looking for. **NEVER** tell an interviewer you don't have any failures. As the question notes keep the failures professional or academic. Do not respond with personal flaws. This is a way to guarantee you won't get the job. The failure that you choose should be a one-time event and not one that has happened many times. You may tell the interviewer that you failed to pass your math course the first time you took it. Do not blame the failure on anyone or make excuses for it. Simply tell the interviewer what you failed at and how you responded to that failure. Tell the interviewer, "I failed my stats class the first time I took it. I responded by immediately signing up for the class the next semester. I took what I learned from my first experience and applied it. I also ensured I planned enough time to study and took advantage of study groups the professor had set up. I am pleased to report I earned an A the next time."

6. *Do you enjoy working with a team or alone or tell me about a time when you worked with a team?*

You enjoy working with other people, but you are also self-directed and can work alone as well. Tell about a time that you worked with a team with great results. If you do not have an example from work, bring up a group project in college or during your volunteer work. Always have a "play well with others" story ready.

7. *When have you had a conflict with someone you worked with, and how did you handle it?*

Of course, you are going to have conflicts with people, but the answer here will be an issue-based conflict. You will not say anything negative about any individual you have ever worked with. Mention a time that you disagreed with someone on an issue, and explain how you positively dealt with the issue, but never attack the person. For example, "One conflict situation that I remember at work was when I was assigned to an office that was larger than my coworker's office. He felt that he should have gotten the office because he had been there longer. Actually, it did not matter to me, but it was important to him. Therefore, I just switched offices with him. I think the supervisor thought that he would not want to change offices, so she assigned it to me. It was one of those simple misunderstandings that turned out okay in the end."

You should anticipate follow-up questions that may be aimed to see if you will speak negatively about a colleague or boss. Do not fall for this one. If they follow up by asking about a time when things did not turn out as well, end with something generic such as, "Conflicts will occur, but when you treat people with respect, most of the time you can find a solution that everyone can agree on. I have found that people want to be listened to more than agreed with. I was working for an insurance company and a person was angry because the company did not replace his roof due to hail damage, but only replaced half of the roof. For me to become upset would have escalated the problem. I let him vent his frustrations. Then I said that I could understand his frustration. Unfortunately, the company paid for the claim as stipulated in the policy. I then offered to resubmit the claim. He was not pleased with the results, but he did calm down and left the office feeling better than when he came in." Hopefully, you will not be pressed to tell about a bad result, but in this case, you are not speaking negatively about a colleague, boss, or even a customer.

8. *How are you with working under pressure?*

You are going to say that you work well under pressure and give an example. You may actually work more efficiently under pressure because you feel challenged. You may suggest that you have fantastic time management skills, which reduce the occurrences of stress; however, you can work effectively under pressure. If you crack under stress, do not mention this at an interview, but take courses, read books, attend workshops, and/or listen to tapes to overcome this obstacle.

9. *What if you were asked to do something that you disagreed with?*

This is an easy question to answer. If you were asked to do something that you did not enjoy doing, but it was part of your job description, then you would do it. If you were asked to do something that was unethical, you would explain why you must decline. However, mention that this company has an outstanding reputation and you do not believe that the latter would ever occur.

10. *Why should we hire you over the other qualified applicants who have applied for this position?*

This is not the time to become shy. Explain the traits and skills that a person in such a position should possess and how you are that person. Then reiterate your impeccable work ethic and dedication to the company, colleagues, and clients. Mention your fantastic communication skills such as listening, interpersonal communication, and public address.

11. *Where do you see yourself in five years?*

Do not give the common answer of "I want your job." You would not want to tell them that you will open your own business or will move on from the company to work for a competitor. If you are interested in an administrative position, you can explain that you have set goals for yourself to gain professional development and would like to work to progress professionally in the company. When I moved into my present position, I told the interviewers that I would work to improve my teaching skills to become the best teacher I could be. I do not have a desire to move into administration, but I will work diligently to provide the best learning environment possible for my students. Mention your professional goals such as being in the top 3 percent in sales within the company.

12. *The final question asked is usually, do you have any questions you would like to ask us?*

Be ready to ask appropriate questions. You should not ask about salaries. Look up the salaries from the company Web site or on sites such as Glassdoor. Have an idea about what you may be offered. If you are asked what salary you require, say that salary is negotiable depending on the company standard. If you are pressed forward, you will need to give a range that you will accept. By researching the typical amounts, you can give a range that does not scare the interviewers and that you can be happy with. This is not the time to ask about vacation time, sick leave, or benefits.

The questions that you ask should relate to the company or organization and the specific job for which you are applying. You may ask about specific projects that are presently a priority. You could ask how soon you would begin working if you were offered the job. You may ask about the first project you would be working on if you were offered the position.

End the interview on a positive note and still smiling, no matter what. The search committee may have someone in mind before you came in, and that person may not work out. Even if you feel that they have been negative with you, leave on a positive note with all doors wide open.

In the end, be prepared for standard questions, unique questions, and follow-up questions. Answer each question honestly and with confidence. When you are asked a question, think about your response and then answer, giving examples. You should always be positive and never say anything negative about a former boss, coworker or company. Think about your positive qualities and talents and how these relate to the position that you are seeking. Practice answering questions with family and friends. Interview for a job as you would prepare for a speech: Research, prepare, practice, have a professional appearance, and use immediacy behaviors.

The Follow-up Letter

Immediately after your interview, go home and write individual thank-you notes to each person with whom you interviewed. Each letter to a team of interviewers should be different. If they will be making a decision within the week, you can write the letter on a thank-you card and deliver the thank-you notes to the receptionist the next morning, or you can send an e-mail. If you know that interviews will continue for more than a week, mail your thank-you cards that evening. Be careful to mention each person by their preferred title and that the notes are well written and grammatically correct. If you did not write the names down during the interview, look them up on the company Web site if you are unsure. You will thank each person for his and her time. Mention anything that you forgot and wished you had mentioned. Look up examples of thank-you letters online.

When I applied for the job that I am presently working, I forgot one of the person's names on the committee. Thankfully, I had introduced myself to the division administrative assistant and had established a rapport with her, while I was waiting to be called in for my interview. I called her that afternoon and told her that I wanted to be sure to include everyone in the thank-you notes that I was writing. She was most helpful in providing me with the names and correct titles of each person. The next morning I delivered my thank-you notes for each interviewer and a special card for her. I personally told her how much I appreciated her assistance and how she made this experience as pleasant as it could be. Within the other notes, I mentioned specific concerns that the individual interviewers had expressed. I had had one of the faculty members on the team in a class ten years prior. I expressed my appreciation for the difference she had made in my life then, and what an honor it would be to work with her, again.

Take this final interviewing step seriously. Even if you are no longer interested in the job after the interview, write a note thanking the interviewers for their time. People talk, and if your name comes up, it should be in a positive context. After you write your notes, letters, or e-mails, ask someone to proofread what you have written. Your writings should be positive, professional, personable, and grammatically correct.

If you are the person doing the hiring, provide each person that you interview with a follow-up letter. Those who have made it to the interview are potential employees and may be the people who will be working with your competitors. After you have made your decision, follow up with a thank-you note for that person's time and let him or her know that you keep applications on file for a specific period of time, if another opening comes up in the near future. Interviewing is a laborious task for the job seeker and the employer. Those who reached out to you in the process may be a potential employee that you would consider later. A note will help in keeping lines of communication open for promising future prospects.

Phone Interviews

If you are applying for a position outside of your local area, you may be called upon to have a first interview over the telephone. Prepare for such an interview in the same way that you would a face-to-face interview. You will research the company, prepare for questions, and take the call on time. Be sure to be free from distractions. I would suggest using a landline and not a cell phone that may lose a connection. Use immediacy behaviors, even on the telephone. This may sound strange, but people on the other line can hear a smile. Lean forward, be prepared and practiced, and do not read your responses. Also, be cognizant of distractions such as background noise, vocalized pauses, tag questions, jangling jewelry, monotone voice, and self-criticism. I interviewed someone on the phone who was obviously reading his responses, which made him appear to be an inept communicator. He also read some of the history of the college straight from our Web site. Another phone interview, where the person used many vocalized pauses was so distracting that it was difficult to listen to the answers to the questions.

Answers on the phone should be as clear and concise as possible. If you do not understand the question, ask the interviewer to repeat the question or rephrase the question, and ask for clarity. As with the face-to-face interview, always be positive, let the interviewer know why you are the most qualified person for the position, and ask appropriate questions when asked to do so. The telephone interview is designed to give the interviewers enough information to decide if they want to spend the time and money to bring you to the area for a face-to-face interview. You should do extra research on the area. Express why you have a desire to move to this location. If you are applying outside of your region, your cover letter should explain why you are interested in a move. This may include that you have family in the area or that you were originally from this location or that you have heard about promising opportunities in a career that encompasses your dream job. In the phone interview, let the interviewers know how much you look forward to meeting them face-to-face.

If you have already visited the area, tell them how excited you would be to relocate to the area because of a pastime that the area is known for or because of the warm people that you have met there. If you have not visited the city, let the interviewer(s) know of your research about the area and why you believe that you will enjoy living there. Relocating is a major step. Explain why you are willing to make the move and stay with them for an extended period of time. Remember to send those important follow-up thank-you cards, letters or e-mails.

If a phone interview is successful and you are asked to come to another location for a face-to-face interview, you have wowed the interviewer(s). The interview at the next level, on their turf, should be just as impressive. Remember to prepare, practice, look professional, display immediacy behaviors, arrive early, ask appropriate questions, and send thank-you notes afterward. Yes, a second thank-you note or follow-up letter is a good idea. The face-to-face after a phone interview is most exciting, so be ready to impress.

Turning People Down

I would suggest that you go to every interview in which you are invited. I have gone to interviews for jobs that I did not plan on accepting, but wanted the experience. You should never admit this when you are in an interview, but trial runs are helpful. You may send out several applications. When researching the company to prepare for the interview, you may discover that the job is not what you are looking for, or during the interview you may get the sense that this is not the company where you would be a good fit. The interview is not only an exploration of the company discovering if they want you to work for them, but it is also for you to discover if you will want to work for them. After all, you do not want to accept a position that will put you on a job hunt next month with a lapse in employment on your resume. If you are offered a job in a company that you do not want to accept, you need to decline most diplomatically. When you go to an interview, you have taken the time of important people within the company who are coworkers of people within your field. How do you turn people down in such a situation? Gently.

When I obtained my undergraduate degree in communication, I sent out applications, resumes, and cover letters to about fifty employers. My first interview was with a local newspaper. I did my research and practiced answering interviewing questions. It was a fantastic experience to speak with the executive marketer, editor, and sales executive of my local paper during the interview. When they explained that the job entailed advertising sales on a commission basis, I knew that this was not the position that I would be happy doing for a long period of time. I completed the interview on a positive note, and sent personal thank-you cards to each person on the interviewing committee. The executive marketing administrator called me and offered me a position. I explained how it was such an honor to meet him and the other people who had interviewed me. I was a fan and subscriber to the newspaper, but I was looking for a career that was not commission based for my pay. My degree was in public relations, and I was searching for a job where I could create a variety of documents such as annual reports, advertisements, speeches, and work in media relations rather than concentrating on sales and advertising. He understood and did not want to hire someone who would be searching for another job while working for him. Six months later, I finally obtained the job I really wanted. Ironically, I ended up working with the local paper and the people in that interview when I sent out media releases, during public meetings and when preparing advertisements. Always be honest and optimistic.

If you are an interviewer, you will also have to turn people down. The last search committee that I had the opportunity to work on had more than fifty qualified applicants. We conducted four interviews. It was a time-consuming and important task. There were five people on the committee. Those who came to the interviews had impressive qualifications, resumes, and cover letters. Although the person chosen was most impressive, it was heartbreaking to turn the others down. Fortunately, I did not have to speak with those who did not get to join our team. However, our human resources officer sent each person a letter in a prompt manner so these individuals knew that another person had been hired.

The key to turning someone down who has applied with your company is adhering to the golden rule: Turn someone down as promptly and respectfully as you would want to be informed if you were searching for a job. If the person who applied contacts you personally to discover why you chose someone else, be honest. If you know of another company or organization where she can apply, reveal this information. Being turned down after an interview is difficult. If you must have the confrontation, let the person know his strengths and opportunities for improvement.

For example, if a person that you interview with has the degree and communication skills that were what you required but lacked experience, let him know and suggest ways to obtain experience. If you are turned down for an interview and the person who interviewed you was approachable, call that person back and ask for feedback and leads that you can pursue.

Summary

Interviewing is important throughout one's career. This chapter explained the significance of presenting well in a job interview, scholarship interview, and when conducting an interview. Preparing for the interview includes researching companies or organizations, job descriptions, and salary scales. Understanding and implementing proper introductions and nonverbal communication make a good first impression. Be prepared to answer questions in your interviews. You should research the company and be prepared to answer typical interview questions as well as follow-up questions. Answer interview questions honestly and give examples where you have had experiences that describe your talents, skills, and proficiencies in the job duties. If you are asked to interview for a job, you already have the qualifications for the career you are seeking, so be prepared to impress by looking professional. It is also important that interviewees know what questions to ask at the end of the interview and follow up with a thank-you letter. Example questions have been provided, but read books and articles that will prepare you for the interview. I would suggest that the job seeker also review resume examples online and in articles and books to develop a resume that will get you noticed. Ask a friend who works in your field of study to carefully review your resume. Create a cover letter to accompany your resume that highlights your qualities that is specific to the company or organization where you would like to work. If you are asked to interview over the telephone, prepare, practice and eliminate distractions.

Although students who read this chapter will be preparing to interview for a job and/or scholarship opportunity, they will also interview others throughout their professional careers. Managers who are not successful in interviewing others lose credibility with potential employees and may not recruit the best team members to a company. Nonetheless, employers who consider the interviewing process, questions to ask when interviewing, and how to turn down applicants during the interviewing processes can recruit and retain a team that is most effective.

Activities

1. Consider the job that you would like to obtain. Write at least ten traits that comprise a successful, efficient, and effective person in this field. Write a philosophy statement that incorporates these traits. This is a difficult task, but considering your talents as it relates to your career should be thoroughly considered before your job interview. An example is provided below.

As a college professor, I believe that I must be **confident, knowledgeable, and understandable** in order to empower my students to learn communication skills that will enhance their lives. In helping them learn these valuable skills, it is important that I model **exemplary interpersonal and professional communication skills** in my classes.

Successful instructors must demonstrate **immediacy behaviors.** This includes addressing students by name, responding to all correspondences in a timely manner, providing encouragement and specific areas to improve when grading student work, and being **positive** and **caring** when responding to questions, posts, and e-mails. I should **require students to meet high standards** in order to master the needed skills, but positive and **honest** communication provides the most meaningful learning environment. I am **open-minded** to student evaluations because my students' suggestions for improvement are most helpful to my professional growth.

As a student of andragogy, I believe that I am to assist my students in understanding the need-to-learn communication skills in their personal and professional lives. I must also engage them in the learning process. It is important to allow students to discuss the information in class. However, it is also essential that a professor maintains a sense of control in the class to avoid class time being wasted by the unruly student. In other words, professors should be caring, **cooperative**, and encourage student input, while maintaining a sense of **structure**. In order to assist adult students I must be a **life-long learner** in my field, provide **clarity** when explaining concepts, explain how the information is useful to their lives, and be **respectful**. My lectures, assignments, exams, and discussions must be useful and assess student learning while providing honest, meaningful, and immediate feedback.

2. Research a company or organization.

    A. Brief history about the company.

    B. Find a job description that you would like to obtain that is posted on the company or organization's Web site or look up job descriptions from another source. Write the job description.

    C. How do your skills match those in the job description?

    D. What are the mission and vision statements of this organization?

E. Write a cover letter. This should explain what job you are
    interested in, how you discovered there was a job opening,
    the skills that you have that match what the organization
    needs or has been listed in an ad, and in the job description.
    Then you will check back in a few days to see if they received
    your resume and references.

3. Write answers to each of the questions. Be sure to give specific
    examples where applicable.

    A. *Tell us a little about yourself.*

    B. *Tell us about the professional experience that you have as a
        _____ (insert job).*

    C. *What are your three greatest strengths or what would you
        suggest is your greatest strength?*

D. *What is your greatest weakness?*

E. *Tell me about a time when you failed. What did you learn from this?*

F. *Do you enjoy working with a team or alone?*

G. *When have you had a conflict with someone you worked with, and how did you handle it?*

H. *How are you with working under pressure?*

I. *What if you were asked to do something that you disagreed with?*

J.   *Why should we hire you over the other qualified applicants who have applied for this position?*

K.   *Where do you see yourself in five years?*

L.   *Do you have any questions you would like to ask the interviewers?*

References

Beatty, R. H. (2003). *The interview kit* 3rd ed. New York: John Wiley and Sons.

Beebe, S. A., Beebe, S. J. & Ivy, D. K. (2006). *Communication: Principles for a lifetime*. Boston: Pearson Custom Publishing.

Bolles, R. N. (2008). *What color is your parachute? A practical manual for job-hunters and career-changers*. Berkeley, CA. Ten Speed Press.

DeVito, J. A. (2006). *Human communication: The basic course* 11th ed. Boston: Pearson Education.

Higgins, M. (2013, May 28). Using the Star technique to shine at job interviews: a how-to guide. *The Guardian*. Retrieved from http://careers.theguardian.com/careers-blog/ star-technique-competency-based-interview

Michael, P. (2007, Oct. 4). How to answer 23 of the most common interview questions. *Wise Bread*. Retrieved from *http://www.wisebread. com/how-to-answer-23-of-the-most-common-interview-questions*

Taylor, J. & Hardy, D. (2005). *Monster careers: Interviewing*. New York: Penguin Books.

Chapter Seven

Listening for Success

The objectives of this chapter are to:

- ✓ Understand the importance of listening.
- ✓ Define listening.
- ✓ Examine how to break bad habits of listening.
- ✓ Comprehend reasons to listen.
- ✓ Incorporate attentive listening.
- ✓ Interpret message content.
- ✓ Interpret emotional meaning.
- ✓ Understand the listening process.
- ✓ Remember information.

Communication researchers and educators agree that listening is a skill that is essential to learning and to being a competent communicator (Bostrom & Waldhart, 1988; Elkeles, 2001; Evers, Rush & Berdrow, 1998). In fact it is the most used skill in communication. According to Colleen McKenna (1998), we spend 80 percent of our day listening and 40 to 80 percent of our salary is earned by listening. Consider the importance of listening in most or any professional occupation.

- Doctors in making diagnoses
- Nurses in being able to serve their patients
- Salespeople and marketing professionals in understanding the needs of clients
- Educators in assessing student understanding
- Criminal justice professionals to gather information
- Journalists during interviews
- Personnel managers to find the best person for a job or promotion
- Attorneys to comprehensively understand the point of view of clients
- Computer analysts to gather user requirements
- Psychologists and psychiatrists meeting the needs of their patients
- Social workers in working with the people they assist
- Researchers when making observations and gathering data from participants
- Administrative assistants to relay messages and follow directions
- Managers in communicating with employees and customers
- Leaders of nonprofit organizations to pinpoint needs of community

- o Customer service professionals to adequately assist clients
- o Servers to get the correct orders
- o And any other occupation where you work with others.

Listening is an essential skill in any profession and relationship, yet it is the least taught skill at any educational level.

Defining Active Listening

The International Listening Association defines listening as, "An active process of receiving, constructing meaning from, and responding to spoken and or nonverbal messages" (ILA, 1996). If effective listening is implemented, the receiver of the message will hear the entire message and respond to the sender that the message has been heard effectively (Evers, Rush, & Berdrow, 1998). Mead and Rubin (1985) suggest that listening skills also include analysis and synthesis as well as nonverbal listening where the listener derives meaning from nonverbal cues such as voice tone, expressions, and gestures. It is an active process. Margarete Imhof (Wolvin, 2010) defines the complexity of listening versus hearing.

> Listening involves processing information from various internal and external sources, as the verbal information may be complemented and modified by prior knowledge, context information, situational variables, body language, and nonverbal paralinguistic messages. While hearing, which is a necessary precursor of listening, occurs automatically, listening is an intentional and controlled process which requires attentional capacity, expends energy, depletes self-regulatory strength, and requires information processing across several modalities, such as acoustic and visual signals. (p. 98)

Active listening is a choice of taking in verbal and nonverbal stimuli, considering the content and situational conditions, constructing bridges from what we know to new information, to comprehend, providing feedback to the source, maintaining an open posture, and resisting physical and psychological noise. No wonder you are exhausted after a day of lectures, meetings, or training sessions. Listening is not an activity that you can be fully immersed in while working on something else.

It is better to give the speaker your full attention for five minutes than twenty minutes of unfocused hearing. Listening is not a multitasking event.

Breaking Bad Habits

Evaluate the last time you listened for thirty minutes or more at work, with a friend, and with a family member. Did you make eye contact, give the person your undivided attention, turn off the television or stay away from the computer, maintain open posture, and focus on the other person instead of yourself? If you are actively listening, you engaged in the communication event. To master the art or skill of listening, it is essential that we break the bad habits we have developed and build upon the positive skills that we possess. In general, people are egocentric. We tend to listen by concentrating on our past experiences, our need to know the information, our judgments of others, and our desire to simply solve the problems of others and move on. To listen, you must decide to be interested and remain calm. If you are experiencing any other emotions besides interest and calm, such as boredom, anger, excitement, or fear, listening ability is strongly impeded.

The One-up Story

A colleague tells you about a problem that he/she is having. As you listen you begin thinking about a past experience when you were faced with the same problem. Your mind wanders back at that time as you begin formulating your one-up story. Then you dive into the story that you developed, which is more dramatic than the problem of your friend. This is a bad habit.

One day a colleague told me that she had an injury that required physical therapy. She was struggling with keeping up with career and family responsibilities, while spending an exorbitant amount of time in therapy. She needed me to listen, not share an irrelevant experience. As soon as she mentioned physical therapy, my mind trailed off to the time when my son had an injury and went to three physical therapists that did not help him. I had the one-up physical therapy story. Then I thought about how my past experience or the advice that I may want to offer was irrelevant; she needed me to listen and understand. In such a situation, keep the conversation on the person's need who is talking to you. Do not divert the conversation to your experience. Let the conversation evolve so the individual can express needs, concerns, and solutions. Encourage the speaker to continue by maintaining open posture, asking relevant questions about her or his story, and being silent to encourage the speaker to continue (Blodgett, 1997).

Concentrating on Our Need to Know the Information

Adults tend to tune into information that they believe meets their immediate need to know. This can be helpful for instructors to know when creating lessons, but it can work against us when actively listening to others. Consider a time when you were discussing a topic that was important to the source but not a topic that you perceived as important to your personal goals. For example, your significant other wants to discuss a problem that she is having with a family member. The family member in the conversation is someone that you avoid. The conversation does not directly affect you; therefore, you allow your mind to wander. To assist you in listening more empathically, try to consider the need of the person who is confiding in you at the time. Although the topic is boring to you, it is important enough for this person that you care about to take time to discuss it. You should not try to offer a simple solution. Sit back and consider the feelings of the other person. The topic may not be necessary to meeting your goals, but if you are discussing a topic that is important to someone who is important to you, then you should focus on his or her topic.

Our Judgments of Others

We live in a polarized society. We make quick judgments about people and tend to pass judgments on others based on one characteristic of the individual. If a person is of another political affiliation, religion, race, age, or gender than you, these differences do not make the other person ignorant or uncaring. The bipartisan attitudes of some individuals are so emotional that it affects the ability to listen objectively to ideas. Similarly, if a person discovers another person's religious beliefs, it can be a hindrance. There are biases against people who are obese, fast-food employees, smokers, poor, disabled, and the list goes on. Realize that you have biases and this can hinder you from listening to others. However, to marginalize a group of people or intolerance is intolerable.

I prefer to avoid discussing a topic with someone who is overly judgmental and does not respect my opinion. Such conversations end up in heated displays of one person trying to forcefully push information on another. It is counterproductive, leaving both parties frustrated and feeling negatively about the other. In such a case, offensive listening is practiced that skews perception. "Avoid offensive listening, tendency to listen to bits and pieces of information that will enable you to attack the speaker or find fault with something the speaker has said" (Devito, 2009, p. 91). Listen to the entire message before making any judgments. It is okay for a person to disagree with your point of view. Maintain an attitude of respect. If you work to pick a speaker's message apart while they are speaking, you are not listening nor will you understand the message. Take a breath, do not interrupt, and consider their points of view. Do not interpret a message to fit your biases. You can disagree with an open mind.

If you are in a situation where you must speak with someone who is judgmental, avoid becoming defensive. This is not to say that you should listen to insults. However, the best way to diffuse a potential argument is to stay calm. You do not have to defend yourself and explain your values, beliefs, or attitudes if you believe you are right. Tom Lewis and Gerald Graham (2003) suggest that if you are spending time defending your position, you are not listening. Instead, listen to the other person's position and let that person know that you understand her or his point of view; you just disagree on this one issue.

Our Desire to Simply Fix the Problem and Move On

We live in a fast-paced society. The people on sitcoms solve their family problems in seventeen minutes or less. We expect to receive our food within minutes after ordering, connect to Internet sites around the world in moments, and solve problems within a few minutes. Listening to another person's problems is not the most pleasant of situations. Nonetheless, the tendency to give a simple reply to fix the problem is not welcome. In fact, when people are discussing a problem, you should not offer advice unless asked. Listen and respond with feedback that shows that you are listening. Rather than offering advice, try to consider the feelings of the other person.

Deborah Tannen (1990) suggests that men and women communicate differently. Women think on a relationship level and communicate to establish rapport. Men think more on a content level and communicate to report. This is not to say that either approach to communication is wrong, just different. It is important that both sexes understand the differences to improve relationships. Men tend to interject knowledge and expertise. It would be more effective to listen to the full explanation and allow the speaker to consider solutions on her own. Women tend to speak about relationships with others and compare their relationships and experiences in conversation. Both approaches can hinder communication. If men and women are cognizant of the differences, it will enhance communication between genders. When speaking with someone about an issue, consider the content and relationship levels of the conversation. Ask questions that will encourage the other person to discover his or her own solutions. Only offer advice when and if asked.

Why We Tune In and Tune Out

We selectively take in information. In other words, we make a choice to tune in to a message or we decide to tune out. It is difficult to actively listen for long periods of time. It takes discipline and determination. There are many reasons for tuning in and tuning out. Eight of the reasons that we actively listen are listed below.

> *You admire the person speaking.* If you choose to listen to others, you are giving them a type of power. You are therefore going to tune in more to people that you respect, admire, like, trust, and are entertained by (Hamlin, 2006). Conversely, you will tune people out who are aloof, negative, or are telling you something that you perceive is meaningless.

> *Interest in the topic.* It is obvious that you tune in more to topics of interest. When we are listening to a lecture about a topic that we do not see as relevant or interesting, it is difficult to stay focused. In these cases, try to seek out novel

information. If the information that you perceive as boring is from a person that you care about, realize that this will assist you in gaining a better understanding of this person.

Get upset. There may be topics that evoke negative emotions. Try to realize that it is not essential that others agree with you. Respectfully listen to conversations with which you do not agree.

Do not comprehend the meaning of words or phrases. "We put on the brakes when we hit an unintelligible word-snag, we lose concentration, and we also lose the momentum built up by the speaker" (Hamlin, 2006, p. 69). As a speaker, use familiar words; as a listener, ask questions if you do not know the meaning of a word or phrase.

Feelings of equality. According to researchers, doctors interrupt patients on an average of eighteen seconds into the first conversation. Less than 2 percent of these patients completed their statements after the interruption (Osborne & Ulrich, 2008, p. 2). Interrupting rather than thoughtfully listening sends a message that you feel superior to the person you are speaking with, and his or her thoughts and feelings are not of value to you. Respect for the other person will assist you in becoming an active listener.

Worry or anxiety. If you are absorbed in personal concerns, it will be difficult to pay attention. You must realize that you are preoccupied and consciously determine to set aside your worries.

Daydreaming. People speak at about 125 words a minute, but our mind can process 1,200 words per minute (Beebe, Beebe & Ivy, 2007). This provides downtime that can lead to our minds wandering in different directions. Avoid daydreaming by focusing on the verbal and nonverbal messages being sent. Also, focus on reading the emotional content of the message. Maintain an open posture and avoid distractions. If you are listening to a lecture, taking notes that pull out the main points and terms will help keep you focused. Focusing your mind on the message will assist you in avoiding daydreaming.

Time. Are you a morning or an evening person? Plan your day to have the most intense communication events at the times that you are most alert. My husband and I are not morning people. We do not try to communicate with one another until we have had a cup of coffee. Our best conversations are in the evenings when we get home from work.

Listening Attentively

Listening attentively involves focus, open posture, and empathy. Make an attempt to concentrate on the verbal and nonverbal messages. If you think that you may not understand the message, ask questions or paraphrase what has been said. The questions should be specific, but do not put the person on the defensive. You should also practice paraphrasing or rephrasing the statements to confirm your understanding.

When you are actively listening, you should look the part. Make eye contact; face the person with whom you are speaking. Lean forward. Provide the speaker with appropriate feedback. Avoid expressions or sounds that would dissuade the person from completing his or her thoughts. Attentive listening means that you give the person your undivided attention. Eliminate distractions. People know if you are splitting your attention. "If you are tempted to split your attention between listening and something else, ask yourself whether you can risk appearing disinterested and the negative impression that it is likely to make on them" (Wilson, 2005, par. 10). Act like you care about the person speaking and the content.

Empathic listening is when you make a sincere effort to imagine the feelings of the other person. Number five of Stephen Covey's (1997) *Seven habits of highly effective families* is "Seek first to understand . . . Then to be understood." By empathically listening, you are seeking to understand. You display caring. If you first seek to understand, then you earn the right to be understood. Keep conversation about the topic the speaker needs to discuss. Transition before changing topics, making sure that the person does not feel that you have ended the conversation abruptly.

Silence is a way to encourage the speaker to continue. Instructors who ask questions of students should remain silent and allow the student to consider the question. Be careful to not interrupt. Researchers (Johnson, Pearce, Tuten, & Sinclair, 2003) conducted an interesting experiment on self-imposed silence to improve listening skills. Participants went twelve hours, while communicating with other people, and did not speak for the entire twelve hours. They could use nonverbal communication and write messages, but were not to speak. They were also to keep journals about the experience. If they broke their silence, the participants would start again with another twelve hours of silence. This significantly enhanced the participants' listening skills and awareness about personal listening behaviors. One of the journal entries was, "People tell you more and give more information when they know you are really listening and won't be cutting in" (p. 7). As an extrovert, being silent takes effort, but it is a helpful exercise to make one more aware of personal listening behaviors.

Attentive listening requires skill and practice. Productive, meaningful, and honest conversation cultivates teamwork within organizations (Donoghue & Siegel, 2005). Take a day to work on your listening skills. Try being silent for at least a few hours. Focus on understanding the complete message when attending to others. Use open posture, even if you do not feel like listening. Make an effort to understand the feelings of others.

Rules for Conversation

Within our culture, we have established rules for respectful conversations. Remember the rules that you would like others to follow are the rules that you should follow as well. Although there are thousands of social norms and rules that we have established in our culture during conversations, below is a list that should be adhered to during all conversations.

○ Conversations are two-way. Take turns.
○ Do not interrupt.
○ Always speak respectfully.
○ Be honest. Do not exaggerate or be misleading.
○ Organize your thoughts and be succinct.
○ Be sincere in your delivery.
○ Provide feedback to the speaker.
○ Use vocal variety to set the mood of the conversation.
○ Be sure that the other person has time to spend.

Before the conversation begins, ask if the person has time, and you may want to ask for a specific amount of time. Listen carefully, and do not give advice unless you are asked. To maintain the trust of others, you should be honest. Do not waste the time of those who choose to listen to you. Say what you mean so others can follow your ideas. It is difficult to listen to someone who is speaking in a monotone voice. Use vocal variety when you speak as the sender of the message and when providing feedback as a listener.

Ask Questions

The book *Communication: Principles for a lifetime* (Beebe, Beebe & Ivy, 2007) lists four reasons for why we ask questions.

> *1) To obtain additional information; 2) To check how a person feels; 3) To ask for clarification; 4) To verify that you have reached an accurate conclusion about your partner's intent or feeling. (pp. 125–126)*

If you need additional information to fully understand the message, ask. People enjoy talking about themselves. Ask questions to encourage self-disclosure. Ask how the individual feels about what is being discussed. You should be specific and acknowledge the other person's feelings. If you do not understand something that has been said, ask for clarification. If you become upset about something the speaker has said, clarify that you comprehend the meaning of the message. If you are discussing an issue or negotiating, summarize the conclusion to the issue. You may paraphrase the message to clarify that you understand.

Interpreting a Variety of Nonverbal Cues

The majority of messages received are nonverbal. Nonverbal communication includes gestures, facial expressions, postures, space or proxemics, touches, paralanguage or the rate, tone, and pitch of our voices (Heathfield, 2010). There are many pieces of data that we process during a typical conversation and plenty of opportunities for misunderstandings. Make an effort to consider nonverbal communication when you are listening to others. It takes effort and practice, but will become a habit after you practice over and over. Questions to consider when interpreting nonverbal communication include:

o   Do the speaker's body movements match the words of the speaker?
o   Does the speaker display an open posture?
o   What are the tone, rate, and pitch of the speaker's voice?
o   In what zone of proxemics is the speaker?
o   At what point does the speaker show a desire for feedback?

As you listen, consider if the speaker is facing you, making eye contact, leaning forward. Does the speaker's posture match the message? You intuitively take in nonverbal cues when you communicate with others. To improve on interpreting these communication behaviors, start by consciously watching and evaluating. It is also important that you work on improving your nonverbal communication. A heightened awareness of your nonverbal cues will assist you in reading the nonverbal communication of others. An activity at the end of this chapter provides a checklist that you will complete after three different communication events. You will assess your gestures, posture, eye contact, and affect displays. This will be beneficial when you attempt to understand the meanings of these nonverbal behaviors in others.

Interpreting Message Content

To interpret messages, one will listen for main ideas, critically listen to the content, and avoid distractions. As a student of public speaking, you have learned to develop an outline that emphasizes your main points. You also transition from one main point to another. Use this skill when listening to others in a variety of settings. If you are listening to a lecture, work to improve your listening skills by writing down the main points of the lecture. Try to identify the organizational pattern for speeches or lectures. Then write the main points and subpoints. What supporting material is being used to substantiate the information? Does the speaker use research data, stories, testimonies, or illustrations? This will help you to stay focused, even if the topic is not something that you are not motivated to learn.

Although you should listen to the totality of the speaker's argument before making judgments, you should still critically analyze the message (Grice & Skinner, 2007). Consider what parts of the information shared is fact or opinion. Were there fallacies within the argument? Did the speaker use hearsay, or were the points backed up with corroborative evidence from an unbiased source? Do not avoid complex messages or try to oversimplify a message. The critical listener will listen with an open mind, keep biases in check, and evaluate the validity of the message (DeVito, 2006).

Evaluating content involves avoiding internal and external distractions. Focus on the message and do not judge the individual speaking based upon personal appearance. I was waiting for a seat in a crowded restaurant and sat down next to a man who appeared to be a vagrant. I made a judgment that this man would probably start mumbling to himself and that his intelligence level was low. Therefore, I was surprised when he initiated a conversation that was meaningful and enjoyable. I felt ashamed that I had judged this man on appearances alone.

Another area in which we prejudge is if we listen to a topic that we disagree with. If you disagree with the message, you may misinterpret the meaning. Consider the feelings and arguments of others. It is not important that we agree with those we admire; it is essential that we respect those with whom we want to maintain relationships.

To fully comprehend a message, avoid external distractions. This can include noises from a television, others in the room, ringing phones, etc. Turn off as many external distractions as possible so you can focus on the content.

Finally, when listening for content, consider the literal meaning. Sometimes we are looking so closely between the lines that we do not focus on the words that the speaker is saying. Communication occurs within a package of verbal and nonverbal information. Take people at their word and try to understand the message as the speaker meant it. In this way you can listen with an open mind, consider the main points, differentiate fact from opinion, and filter out internal and external distractions.

Interpreting Emotional Meanings

You should consider the emotional meanings when you listen. What is the emotional content within the nonverbal behavior? What emotional elements are driving the conversation? Understanding the emotions of the sender will assist you in reading his or her body language (McKenna, 1998). Consider if the facial expressions show sincere signs of sadness, anger, disdain, disgust, surprise, fear, or interest. These are the eight universal emotions that should look the same on people who are not masking their emotions (Devito, 2006). These facial movements are affect displays and reveal the emotions of the person with whom you are speaking.

Be cautious when reading affect displays. Although the eight universal emotions might be readable, other facial expressions are not. My husband was speaking with me about a trip we were going to take when my mind wandered to a problem that had transpired at work. As I went back to the situation at work, my facial expression turned to what he read as displeasure in his discussion. He then said, "Do you not want to go on this trip?" I then explained what had happened, apologized for my wandering thoughts, and we got the conversation back on track. Remember that the affect displays may not always be related to what you are talking about if the person has momentarily zoned you out.

Paralanguage or rate, tone, and pitch can be helpful when considering the emotional meaning of a message. What is the emotional tone in the speaker's voice? People who are speaking loudly may be upset, trying to be domineering, or are excited about the information. Those who are speaking at a low volume may be sad, shy, or lacking confidence. Speaking at a fast rate may be because the person is from a part of the country when they speak at a higher rate of speed. Speakers who talk fast may also feel rushed, nervous, or excited. Those who speak at a slower rate of speed may also be nervous, unsure of themselves, or from regions of the country where people speak at a slower rate of speed. If you are excited, happy, or nervous, you speak at a higher pitch than when you are sad, bored, or relaxed. Listen to the emotional tone that is displayed through paralanguage to fully comprehend the emotional meanings.

Understanding the Listening Process as It Relates to Communication

Joseph A. Devito (2006) provides a five-step process of listening: receiving, understanding, remembering, evaluating, and responding. This corresponds with the International Listening Association's definition of listening, "An active process by which you receive, construct meaning from, and respond to spoken and or nonverbal messages" (ILA, 1996). We take in messages through our five senses: what we see, hear, taste, smell, and feel. This is done selectively or by consciously listening with our eyes, ears, and heart. Then we strive to understand the messages, building bridges from our past experiences or knowledge to the new information, we are processing. At this point in the process, it is important to consider the message through the sender's point of view. This is also the stage in which you ask clarifying questions and paraphrase the information to make sure that you understand (Devito, 2006).

To remember the information for future recall, one must be able to identify main points and review the information over and over. That is why it is important for speeches and lectures to reiterate the main points in the introduction, body, and conclusion of a presentation. Evaluation of a message is a critical analysis of the message, but it also entails evaluating your perceptions of the message and the messenger. Be aware of your biases that inhibit your understanding of the message that the sender intends to convey.

Finally, the International Listening Association definition agrees with DeVito's (2006) process in that listening includes responding. Active listening will evoke a response. The response can be in the form of back-channeling, where you respond verbally without the desire to take the role as a speaker. These responses include phrases such as, "yes," "I see," "that must have been frustrating," or "I understand that you are upset." Do not use the hurry-up-and-shut-up response of continual, "uh-huhs." Instead, listen intently and provide the sender with an honest, thoughtful response. This may include advice, if advice has been requested. But a response should show your understanding of the message and meet the needs of the sender.

Understanding the process of listening is helpful in understanding the complexities of a skill that is overlooked in educational institutions. When you are engaged in the process, realize that you take in information through your five senses selectively. You strive to understand the information based upon prior knowledge. Then you analyze the data, but you should work to evaluate the information with an open mind. If your prior analysis of information does not match a well-constructed argument, reevaluate. Then ethically respond to the message.

Remembering Information

When we are listening to information in a speech, lecture, or conversation, we want to remember or recall the messages. Unfortunately, recall does not happen without work, unless you have a photographic memory. That is why I have devoted a section to remembering information even though it is part of the process of listening provided by Devito (2006). Pearson, Nelson, Titsworth, and Harter (2008) identified three types of memory: working memory, short-term memory, and long-term memory.

Working memory is when one takes in information and tries to construct meaning of the information. As you selectively receive new information, you will search for patterns and link the unfamiliar to something familiar to you. After you arrive at a meaning of the information, it will go to short-term memory. Your short-term memory has a limited capacity. The best way to retain information that you hear is to rehearse the information. Then, if you can move information to long-term memory, it is yours for a lifetime. However, you will not be able to recall the information unless you have filed it in a place where you can remember. So information is selectively received. Then you consider the relevance of the information to decide if you have a need to recall it later. If you believe that the information is important to you, then you will try to consider the new information as it relates to something that you already know. If you can build a bridge from the known to the new concept, you are more apt to understand and recall the information. With a clear understanding and repetition, you will move the information to long-term memory for future recall.

Memory requires repetition. I started college at the age of thirty. I do not have a photographic memory and have difficulty memorizing data. The way that I could recall information for tests is by working every day with the information provided in lectures. If you are learning a process or concept, write the steps, definitions, or concepts. Then read your notes daily. This takes discipline, but if learners will set aside time *every day* to read over the notes that they have taken, it is possible to move the information into long-term memory and store the information for later recall.

Summary

Listening is the most used skill in communication but the least taught. "The most neglected language arts skill at all education levels is listening" (Wolvin & Coakley, 1996, p. 33). This chapter addressed the importance of learning active listening and provided direction for active listening in a variety of communication situations. To actively listen, one must take in verbal and nonverbal messages, interpret the messages, and remember and respond to the message. Listening is an active process that must be understood and taken seriously in order to improve.

Consider the following example of a positive learning experience. While rushing through your list of essential to-dos left over from yesterday, a pop-up appears on your computer: "Monthly meeting in ten minutes." You grab your legal pad and pen and write one goal that you want to achieve from the meeting. Sitting close to the front of the room, you listen attentively and jot down a question you would like clarified. You notice the speaker appears to want feedback, so you wait for a pause and ask your question. After a few minutes your mind begins to head back to the office without you, but you quickly realize the problem and refocus your attention on the speaker. Due to your newfound listening skills, you realize that your manager is about to ask you a question regarding the project you have just been working on. You listen to the question and respond with a strong answer that pleases your manager. When the meeting adjourns, you go back to your list of to-dos with a better understanding of your coworkers.

Listening skills will deteriorate if you don't use them every day. So while the example takes place in a workplace, these skills apply to any aspect of your life in which listening is important. So make it a practice to use strong listening skills in every facet of your life.

Activities

Self-Assessment of Listening Behaviors

Below is a self-assessment of active listening behaviors. Complete this after three different communication events. Then fill it out for someone else after they have communicated with you. After this event, do you pay more attention to the nonverbal messages from others?

Behavior	Effective	Need to Improve	Comments
Maintained an open posture			
Did not interrupt			
Smiled			
Nodded head			
Maintained eye contact			
Leaned forward			
Sat close enough to the speaker			
Avoided distractions			
Considered nonverbal cues of the speaker			
Listened for emotional meanings			
Considered feelings of the speaker			
Listened to understand or empathically listened			
Asked clarifying questions			
Provided positive feedback			

Silence is Key

The activity below is taken from the research of (Johnson, Pearce, Tuten, and Sinclair (2003) where the participants were silent for twelve hours.

Converse with a partner for thirty minutes. During this time, a partner will talk about himself or herself for fifteen minutes. The partner will tell you about his or her major, family, and favorite hobby. The listener will not add any comment, but silently listen. Then the other partner will discuss his or her major, family, and favorite hobbies. Afterward, discuss your feelings about the experience. Consider what you learned about the listening behaviors of each person, the difficulty of remaining silent, and the listening behaviors of you and your partner.

Write a one-page paper about the experience.

> What did your partner discuss?
> What are your feelings about the experience?
> What did you learn about your listening behaviors?
> What did you learn about the listening behaviors of your partner? Was it difficult to remain silent?

References

Barker, L. L. 1988. Listening skills: *Objectives and criterion referenced exercises*. New Orleans: SPECTRA Incorporated.

Beebe, Beebe & Ivy. (2007) *Communication: Principles for a lifetime*, 3rd ed. Boston, MA: Pearson Custom Publishing.

Blodgett, P. C. (1997, July). Six ways to better listening *Training and Development*. 51. N7.

Bostrom, R. & Waldhart E. (1988). Memory models and the measurement of listening. *Communication education 37* (1), 1–13.

Coakley, C. G. & Wolvin, A. D. 1989. Experiential training: Tools for teachers and trainers. New Orleans: SPECTRA Incorporated.

Covey, S. R. (1997). *Seven habits of highly effective families*. New York: Golden Books.

DeVito, Joseph (2006) *Human Communication: The Basic Course*, 11th ed. Boston: Allyn & Bacon/Longman.

DeVito, J. A. (2009). *The interpersonal communication book*, 12th ed. New York: Pearson Education.

Donoghue, P. J. & Siegel, M. E. (2005). *Are you really listening? Keys to successful communication*. Notre Dame, IN: Sorin Books.

Grice, G. L. & Skinner, J. F. (2007). *Mastering public speaking*, 6th ed. New York: Pearson.

Elkeles, C. (2001). Teaching listening skills in the elementary classroom. Articlesforeducators.[Online]Available:*http://www. articlesforeducators. com/general/000001.aspl*.

Evers, R., Rush, J. & Berdow, I (1998*). The bases of competence: Skills for lifelong learning and employability.* San Francisco, CA: Jossey-Bass Publishers.

Hamlin, S. (2006). How *to talk so people listen: Connecting in today's workplace.* New York: Harper Collins Publishers.

Healthfield, S. (2010). Listen with your eyes:Tips for understanding nonverbal communication. *About.com Guide.* Retrieved from *http://humanresources. about.com/od/interpersonalcommunicatio1/a/ nonverbal_com.htm*

Johnson, I. W, Pearce, G., Tuten, T. L. & Sinclair, L. (2003, June). Self-imposed silence and perceived listening effectiveness. *Business Communication Quarterly.* 66.2.

Lewis, T. D. & Graham, G. (2003, Aug.) 7 tips for effective listening: Productive listening does not occur naturally. It requires hard work and practice. *Internal Auditor.* 60.4.

Osborne, C. A. & Ulrich, L. K. (2008, May). Lessons on listening: Techniques to improve your skill as diagnostician, compassionate doctor and manager. *DVM Magazine.* 39.5

McKenna, C. (1998). *Powerful communication skills: How to communicate with confidence.* Franklin Lakes, NJ: Career Press.

Mead, N. & Rubin, D. (1985). Assessing listening and speaking skills. ERIC digest ED263626. ERIC clearinghouse on reading and communication skills. Urbana, IL. [Online] Available: *http://www. ed.gov/databases/ERIC_Digests/ed263626.html.*

O'Brien, L. (2009). *A speaker's resource: Listener-centered public speaking.* New York: McGraw Hill.

Tannen, D. (1990). *You just don't understand: Women and men in conversation.* New York: William Morrow and Company.

Wacker, K. G. & Hawkins, K. (1995) Curricula comparison for classes in listening. *International Journal of Listening*, 9, 14–28.

Watson, K. W., Barker, L. L. & Roberts, C. V. 1989. *Development and administration of the high school Watson-Barker Listening Test*. New Orleans, LA: SPECTRA Incorporated.

Wilson, B. (2005). Part II: How to listen. *BusinessListening.com*. Retrieved from http://www.businesslistening.com/listening_skills-3.php.

Wolvin, A. Listening and human communication in the 21st century. Malden, MA: Wiley-Blackwell.

Wolvin, A. & Coakley, C. G. 1996. *Listening*, 5th ed. Boston, MA: McGraw Hill.

Chapter Eight

The Lecture or Workshop

The objectives of this chapter are to:

- ✓ Understand andragogy techniques.
- ✓ Design objectives that guide your lecture.
- ✓ Relate information with clarity.
- ✓ Incorporate resources to provide credibility.
- ✓ Back up the information provided with examples the audience understands.
- ✓ Employ media such as PowerPoint, pictures, and videos.
- ✓ Develop activities and/or discussions that involve the audience in the experience.
- ✓ Demonstrate immediacy behaviors and effective delivery techniques.
- ✓ Construct an effective summary.
- ✓ Formulate questions that engage the learner.

Professionals in any type of business or organization may be called upon to present a workshop or extensive presentation in order to inform others in their areas of expertise. Teachers in our K-12 education systems are required to study the art of teaching or pedagogy and then take exams to obtain a license to teach; however, college professors and professional trainers are not held to the same standards when teaching others. Teaching adults is different than teaching children. The study of teaching adults is called andragogy. Adults learn differently. Children are required to attend classes every day, and they do not have the same level of experience and expertise that adults bring to a learning environment.

We take in information through our senses or what we see, hear, taste, smell, and touch. A toddler will explore anything that they can pick up and smell, taste, look at, listen to, and feel. They are programming their hard drives. Adults enter the learning environment with a wealth of experiences gained throughout their lives. They can use this knowledge to better understand information received. When adults who have had different experiences are given information, they process this information differently than children.

To obtain the attention of adults, the presenter must explain why the information is important to the learner's goals, bridge the information being taught to knowledge that the learner already knows, and engage the learner in the material. One theory of teaching adults is called constructivism. Constructivistsunderstandthatadultsshouldnotbespoon-fedinformation. Teachers of adults and children are moving away from the model of simply expecting students to sit as sponges, soaking up data. This type of teaching is when the teacher gives students lists of data; students memorize the data and then students show their memorization skills by matching definitions or answering test questions that assess rote memory. Although there may be disagreements that rote memory education is not important in the information age, it does have its place. For example, students in our elementary schools should still memorize their multiplication tables and the rules of grammar. Nonetheless, learners should be given more of a challenge to take in data and construct meaning from that information by building foundational constructs and then creating higher levels of understanding.

Professional and personal life problems cannot be solved by using methods that we learned in traditional elementary education. Such problems can have a variety of outcomes and ways that they can be solved. Consider a problem that you have recently had to solve. You could not solve a life problem with information that you learned on a rote level. Instead, you were faced with a problem that required you to troubleshoot from your previous experiences or the experiences of others. When you were faced with the problem, you considered your past experiences to discover if you had dealt with this type of problem, and use what you learned then to assist you in solving this problem. If you did not have a similar experience from which to draw, you contacted someone else who you thought would have had an experience with the problem.

For instance, when my daughter was a little sassy, I became angry. She was fourteen and had always been polite, so this threw me. As a mother of four children, I had some experience from which to draw. I thought about my reaction to her negative response and realized that I had responded negatively, so the problem could have escalated out of control. I then called my grown daughter, and she told me that I can be domineering in this area, and I should lighten up. There were several alternatives that I could use to solve the problem, but using my past experiences and the advice from my grown daughter, I decided to lighten up. I explained to my, then, fourteen-year-old that I perceived the tone as disrespectful. We made a pact to speak respectfully to each other and discuss disagreements on a more productive level. This is not going to be the only time that we have this problem, but I feel better equipped to find solutions to future situations.

In the end, when you are teaching adults, realize that every person in your audience has had experiences and a level of expertise that you do not have. Also realize that you have knowledge that your audience needs to comprehend that will assist them in reaching their professional and personal goals. Explain the importance of your topic. Introduce an idea and give an example, anecdote, or hypothetical situation that is comprehensible to the adult learner. Engage adult learners by letting them know how the topic affects them and how the objectives will assist them in their professional and personal goals.

When to Lecture

I began college at the age of thirty. I dropped out of high school at the age of fifteen. When I first began my college experience, I was terrified. I attended every class and made an effort to tune into lectures. I believed that my professors would relay the information that would assist me in reaching my goal of obtaining a career in which I could move my children and myself beyond poverty. I had to take a test that placed me in a series of developmental courses in my first semester. Furthermore, I discovered that I had to take courses in subjects that I did not like. I wondered why courses in history and math were in my program of study. After all, I had lived all of the history that I wanted to know about, and I knew how to balance my checkbook. Fortunately, I had professors who understood my need to understand the importance of this information. My history and math classes have assisted me in becoming a better problem solver and to understand the world around me more comprehensively.

If you are a professor, teacher, corporate trainer, manager, computer services employee, volunteer coordinator, researcher, or need to inform others, you will present a lecture, workshop, or informational speech. The lecture is an extensive information speech. It is important that the presenter has thoroughly researched the topic and even has a passion for the subject area. Dr. Dalton Kehoe (2008) wrote an inspiring article about presenting lectures. He suggests that a love for the subject area is essential when giving a lecture. "Like all great gifts, energetic lecturing communicates your love of the subject and it gets your audience to pay attention. From their point of view, your thoughts and your feelings are the lecture. You energize the material" (Kehoe, 2008, par. 6).

A lecture should be conducted when the audience has a need to learn information and the presenter is knowledgeable and passionate about the topic. Lectures take time for preparation and should be well structured. You begin by telling your objectives. The body of your lecture should systematically, enthusiastically, and interestingly present the information. The conclusion is a thorough summary of the content and provides time for questions.

Objectives

Any presentation will begin with an attention grabber and a road map of where your audience will be during your presentation. The introduction of your lecture should introduce the topic and explain the importance of them listening to you because it will be useful in meeting their personal and professional goals. Do not just start giving concepts, points, and research data. If you are going to give a test afterward, you can mention this; however, adult learners will tune in if you explain short-term and long-term needs that will be met by them learning the information that you provide.

After you have given the audience an attention grabber and the need to listen, you will provide specific objectives that explain what you will be discussing or what they will learn. Think about the main points that you will discuss, and write essential skills and knowledge that you will explain throughout your presentation.

While considering your objectives you should review a list of Bloom's Taxonomy. In developing objectives, your overall goal should be assisting students in moving from basic knowledge of the information to being able to apply the concepts. Below is a list of Bloom's Taxonomy provided by Richard C. Overbaugh and Lynn Schultz (n. d.) from Old Dominion University. Design your objectives with this progressive ideology in mind. Your introduction, content, summary, and assessments should be based upon the objectives of your lecture.

Remembering: can the student recall or remember the information?	define, duplicate, list, memorize, recall, repeat, reproduce, state
Understanding: can the student explain ideas or concepts?	classify, describe, discuss, explain, identify, locate, recognize, report, select, translate, paraphrase
Applying: can the student use the information in a new way?	choose, demonstrate, dramatize, employ, illustrate, interpret, operate, schedule, sketch, solve, use, write.
Analyzing: can the student distinguish between the different parts?	appraise, compare, contrast, criticize, differentiate, discriminate, distinguish, examine, experiment, question, test.
Evaluating: can the student justify a stand or decision?	appraise, argue, defend, judge, select, support, value, evaluate
Creating: can the student create new product or point of view?	assemble, construct, create, design, develop, formulate, write.

Give your audience a visual list of these objectives and tell them that the goal of this presentation is that they learn each of these ideas. For presenting the information in this chapter, I would provide a PowerPoint overhead that lists the main points of the presentation.

The preface to the lecture is most essential because you explain why the audience should listen, incorporate your expertise in the subject, and provide a preview, which is a step-by-step plan so they can follow you on your journey to understanding. Now we will consider how to relate information so your audience understands.

Relate Information with Clarity

Now that you have given your audience the points that you will convey, reiterate each point with supporting data, illustrations, and transitions to your next objective. When developing your presentation, consider the knowledge that your audience already has about your topic. Build on these foundations. Use words and illustrations that your audience can relate to without wasting their time by speaking on a condescending level. Furthermore, individuals have different learning styles so your presentation should provide elements that include learning experiences for the auditory, visual, and kinesthetic learners. There are a plethora of articles and books written about learning styles. Melissa Kelly (2010) wrote an article that succinctly describes the learning styles and techniques to meet the needs of each.

Learning Styles

Auditory learners enjoy lectures and take in information by listening. It would be helpful for auditory learners to read texts and PowerPoint presentations aloud. These learners should use audio tape recordings of lectures so they can listen to the information again. Visual learners benefit from PowerPoint presentations or videos that provide pictures, main points, graphs, and charts. When preparing your lecture, consider visuals that will assist your audience in developing a mental image that illustrates your points.

Kinesthetic learners need to be involved in the learning experience. "Kinesthetic, also called tactile, learners are those who learn best through touching, feeling, and experiencing that which they are trying to learn. They remember best by writing or physically manipulating the information" (Kelly, 2010, par. 4). Within lectures, it is important to provide auditory learners with lecture material, visual learners with pictorial images, and engage kinesthetic learners in activities such as discussions, hands-on activities, and role play.

The auditory learner should tape lectures, read the texts aloud, and even audiotape texts. Visual learners should read the text. Visual learners should also write notes and even draw pictures to have a visual representation of the information. Download and print PowerPoint slides when provided. Kinesthetic learners should read texts aloud while walking around. If you do not know your learning style, take a learning style assessment. Free assessments are provided online. Conduct an online search to find free learning style assessments. However, consider if you enjoy lectures, take in information visually, or need hands-on experiences and you will have a good idea about your personal learning style.

Familiar Words

You should use familiar language and avoid doublespeak. The purpose of a lecture is not to impress your audience with your extensive vocabulary. The purpose is to teach your audience the information clearly. If you need to include words that the audience is unfamiliar with, give a one-line definition that they would understand. For example, "Active listeners are empathic listeners, or listen while considering the other person's feelings." William Lutz (1990) defined four types of doublespeak: euphemism, jargon, gobbledygook, and inflated language. Euphemisms are when you try to say something that could be offensive without being offensive. "For example, you express your condolences that someone has 'passed away,' because you do not want to say to a grieving person, 'I'm sorry your father is dead'" (Lutz, 1990, p. 2). Unfortunately, sometimes the motivation for the euphemism is to mislead an audience and should be avoided. *Jargon* is language used by a particular professional group of people that others may not understand. For example, communication professionals tend to substitute "comm" for communication or "extemp" for extemporaneous speeches, or "CAT" for communication accommodation theory. Most professions use some form of lingo that would not be understood by everyone.

Gobbledygook is a technique to spout a series of unneeded and hard to understand words together so the audience does not understand what you are talking about. There are many examples of this when leaders find themselves in an uncomfortable situation. I have read textbooks and research articles that take a simple idea and use such difficult terminology that it becomes more difficult to understand than it should be. I do not believe that everyone who uses gobbledygook intend to confuse the audience. This can occur if the person speaking or writing has so much information about the terms that they try to convey information, as if everyone in the audience has studied the concept for decades. Present information in layman's terms. Use easy to understand language and comprehensible sentences. The fourth type of doublespeak defined by Lutz (1990) is inflated language that is designed to make the simple seem remarkable. When you present, explain the need to understand and use the information in an understandable way, and avoid making outlandish claims.

Vivid Language

Vivid language formulates images in the listeners' minds by explaining events and concepts with colorful, pictorial explanations. If I were going to discuss active listening, it would be important to explain what an active listener looks like as in the example below.

> You cannot actively listen and multitask. Active listeners become absorbed in the communication event by leaning forward, looking the person in the eyes, displaying open posture, reading nonverbal cues, and considering the feelings of the speaker. Imagine a time when you tried to multitask and listen. You may have been fiddling with your cell phone or glancing at your computer. Perhaps, while the person talked, you rehearsed what you wanted to say when they finished talking. You are your favorite topic, so avoid pondering your come back story while someone else is talking. Listen attentively with your eyes, your mind, and your understanding.

In other words, paint an image of the idea or concept that you are trying to convey. Allow the listener to conceptualize your examples using vivid language.

Novel Verbs and Phrases

Your language should also use active verbs and avoid the use of clichés. Overused verbs should be replaced with more vivid language. For example, if I said that "he ran through the park," it does not provide the images if I were to substitute *ran* with words such as bolted, jogged, loped, staggered, slithered, or scampered. Use verbs that convey the most vivid message possible. Also, avoid overused phrases or clichés such as "cute as a button" or "dry as a bone." Replace such comparisons with creative metaphors, similes, and other figurative language that are discussed in the Motivational Speech chapter.

Summary

Clear language provides the learner with a better understanding of your concepts. The purpose of a lecture is to assist your audience in learning your objectives. Give brief definitions if you use words that a portion of your audience may not understand. Appeal to the learning styles of your audience. Use familiar words that your audience can relate to. Supply your audience with novel, vivid language that artistically paints the images that draws them into your presentation.

Incorporate Resources to Provide Credibility

If you are teaching about a subject, you should read journal articles and books. Let your audience know about recent research about the topic. Discussing research provides you with credibility. Although you will speak about a subject that you know about, none of us know everything about anything. Textbook authors thoroughly research each chapter. Be sure to give the originators of theories and ideas credit. It is also important to tell the audience experts on the topic, and you may want to refer them to books and research if they would like to do further study. Search databases using key words to discover theorists. If you are not familiar with how to conduct research, librarians will assist you in your academic search.

Back Up Information with Understandable Examples

Lectures that simply give lists of definitions are difficult to follow. Think about each of your main points. You will give definitions to key terms. If you are giving a definition, give a one sentence example. Nonetheless, main points should be supported by illustrations and personal stories. Consider a variety of ways to support your points.

Illustrations

One way to link your information is with an illustration about something that your audience is knowledgeable. I read an article that links the symptoms of Irving Janis' concept of groupthink to the Challenger Disaster. When I bring up the symptoms, I use this extensive illustration so my students can comprehend the symptoms as it relates to a real-life situation. The symptoms are rather hard to fully understand without the use of an illustration. I have provided an example of the use of groupthink with an illustration below.

> *Some of the symptoms of groupthink are feelings of being invulnerable, feeling the group is moral, self-censorship, too much cohesiveness, and out of group stereotyping (Griffin, 1997). The administrators at NASA were experts that are highly respected in all areas of the country. If I worked for NASA, I would tattoo this on my body, would wear clothes with the NASA logo, and would have NASA on my license plate. There is a need for people who work at NASA to feel a part of the membership. That is the organization that took us to the moon!*

> *When Challenger was to launch in 1986, an engineer questioned the decision of NASA administrators. He suggested that there was a flaw in the O-rings and they should not launch with the temperature being lower than during previous launches. For the first time, civilians were to go up in Challenger, and NASA administrators, a group of responsible experts, took offense that their decision was questioned. Of course, the NASA administrators did not want to put anyone in harm's way, but the people within the organization were not willing to question the decisions of the organization. In the end, Challenger launched and seven people died. The theorists of groupthink would suggest that organizations that are too cohesive, feel invulnerable, self censor, believe that they are more moral than others, and stereotype outside groups make poor decisions.*

Illustrations are helpful when describing ambiguous concepts. Such illustrations provide learners with identifiable, understandable examples.

Personal Stories

Another way to bring in supporting materials would be using stories that your audience can relate to. If possible, use humorous stories from your personal experiences. This will help you relate to your audience and make your lecture much easier to remember. The lectures that I can recall from college or in workshops usually include some vivid, humorous stories that I would repeat to my friends. I was inadvertently using a memory technique when discussing the stories professors told with my friends and family members. As you review your main points, think about times when you or someone you know experienced the concept. I use the example below when discussing one reason that we should not criticize ourselves in front of an audience.

When we hear self-criticism, we tend to want to respond back. After all, we frequently self criticize because we are fishing for a compliment. One day, my husband and I were in the car going to the mall. I said, "Gosh, I feel like I am looking so old these days." He said, "Don't we all." Then I made a wrong answer noise and said, "Wrong answer." He said, "What was the question?" So I repeat, "Gosh, I feel like I am looking so old these days." He said, "No baby, You are beautiful!!" Then I said, "Ding, ding, ding!" I reeled in that compliment that I captured with my self-criticism. But when you are in front of an audience, they cannot help you and it only makes the audience feel uncomfortable.

Hypothetical Examples

Hypothetical examples or stories are helpful if you are explaining a difficult concept. If you cannot think of a personal experience, consider a hypothetical example. When explaining that we take in information using our five senses, I describe how a ten-month old child takes in data or information by using his or her five senses.

Think about a ten-month-old baby who picks up an object like a water bottle. The tot will look at, listen to, feel, smell, taste, and drool on the object. We take in innumerable bits

*of information through our senses, and these experiences have
helped us form our knowledge base and our frame of reference.*

Providing an everyday hypothetical illustration assists your audience
in linking your concepts with previous experience.

Ask for Student Input

You could even ask students to share their personal experiences with
the concepts you are discussing. This can be done as a class discussion
or with groups. In this way, the students learn from each other. Never
embarrass audience members, but learners may have experiences that
exceed your experiences. You may plan such discussions throughout
the lecture. When I discuss the concept of self-fulfilling prophecy, I
poll the audience. I ask my students by a show of hands if they believe
that they are bad at math. Then I explain how their negative beliefs
may contribute to their negative perceptions due to the theory of self-
fulfilling prophecy.

> *Your belief that you are inept at math may have started as far
> back as the third grade. You were supposed to be studying for
> your multiplication timed tests, but instead you were playing
> with your GI Joe or playing freeze tag with your friends, or
> playing Super Mario on your computer. You take the timed test
> and don't finish it in the time allotted. You look at your friend
> at the next desk and she finished it before time was called. You
> think, "I stink at math." You may have even had a teacher that
> communicated to you that you were not good at math. You
> internalized those feelings. Then you grew to dislike mathematics
> so you did not study as hard in those classes, had some failures,
> and made up your mind that you are bad at math.*
>
> *If you can add, subtract, multiply, and divide, then you can do
> any math problem. You simply must do one step at a time, find
> out when to do each step, spend some time on homework, and get
> that thought out of your mind that you are bad at math. Use self-
> fulfilling prophecy to your advantage. Go into every class, and
> approach every goal believing that you can succeed, and you will.*

Summary

A lecture will use examples, definitions, illustrations, personal experiences, and hypothetical examples, and draw from the learners' experiences throughout. Your audience makes sense of your new material by linking it to their prior knowledge and experience (Tennant and Pogson, 1995). Review your main points and consider how you can assist your audience in linking the knowledge that they have with the new concept that you are asking them to learn. Use a variety of supporting material throughout your lecture to make the lecture livelier.

Employ a Variety of Media such as PowerPoint Presentations, Models, and Videos

To assist your visual learners, use some type of visuals that list your main points. Some instructors will write main points on the board. As a visual learner, I appreciate overheads and PowerPoint presentations that are aesthetically pleasant. I can remember my college algebra teacher using colored markers to work problems from an overhead projector. She could explain a problem so it made sense, even to those of us who thought we were bad at math. If you are going to write a large quantity of information on the board, then write it out before the lecture is to begin. Writing for long periods of time on a whiteboard means that you are talking to your audience when your back is turned. If you are facing a visual aid, your mouth should be closed. It is harder to understand what you are saying when you are not making eye contact with your audience. Your audience cannot make eye contact with the backside of your anatomy.

PowerPoint or Prezi Presentations

PowerPoint and Prezi programs are simple to use. There are templates provided. Your first slide will be your topic and objective. Your learners should understand the points that you want to make. The next slide will have points about the need for the audience to know the information. Consider how the concepts you share will assist them in meeting their personal or professional goals. Then you will have slides that include your main points and sub-points. You can write the titles of research information or bring in graphs and charts to map your numerical information. Add a picture, model or a visual representation of the information on as many slides as possible. Thoughtfully consider what each slide should contain that will be interesting, informative, aesthetically appealing, and understandable.

The slides should contain about six lines of information. The PowerPoint is to visually highlight your points. Do not write out everything you will say and read it off your slides. If you feel that you must put a long quote on a slide, you may want to let your audience read it themselves. The worst lecture I think I have ever heard was when a person put a word document he had typed on an overhead and read it word for word. He read about seven, single-spaced pages. I could not figure out why he did not just give me a copy of his essay. I can read. If you put the lecture on PowerPoint slides, you will have the same results. Instead, provide your main points and explain the information using illustrations, stories, research findings, and hypothetical situations. You may also want to put key terms and definitions on your PowerPoint slides.

Avoid clutter or information overload when creating your slides. Slides could provide a little animation to make the presentation more interesting, as long as the animation does not become distracting. I used to put only my main points on slides for my Communication Theory class. Students had to present a theory and use a PowerPoint presentation when teaching the theory. Two of the men who were one of the classes are twins. They taught a theory and developed a fantastic PowerPoint to go with their presentation. They took pictures that demonstrated their ideas and put these in the PowerPoint and added animation. It was not cluttered and was very effective. After modeling this example of an interesting PowerPoint, they politely suggested that I use these tools to liven up my PowerPoint presentations. Since then, I have tried to improve my visual aids.

You may also want to use models, pictures, and diagrams to explain your points. Of course, pictures and diagrams can be added to PowerPoint presentations. There are certain topics that we need to see to understand. It would be difficult to teach science classes without pictures and models. If there is any way to show the concept using an object, pictures, or diagram, do so. These are powerful tools for your audience.

Videos are tools that add to your lectures. You can search YouTube to find video recordings that would assist you in making your point. I have used two-minute video recordings of others explaining a concept, just to have a break in the lecture. You can also find movie clips, speeches, commercials, and funny spoofs dealing with the information you are teaching. Video clips are helpful to your visual and kinesthetic learners. You may also want to find out if your library has DVDs that would be helpful. When teaching about special occasion speeches, I show an acceptance speech and a commencement speech. I even like to ask students to evaluate favorite movie speeches. The class will be a buzz when we start discussing favorite movie speeches. Movie or television clips are fun resources when explaining a concept that is played out on the big screen. It is a good idea to only lecture for less than 10 minutes and then switch to a video clip, ask discussion questions, play a game, do an activity, and/or have a role play activity.

Summary

There are a variety of resources to help you get your points across. Provide an environment that is most helpful to your students. PowerPoint and Prezi presentations, graphics, pictures, and video recordings are tools to making your lecture more interesting, interactive, and meaningful. It takes time to learn how to use Prezi and PowerPoint programs but is worth the investment. Search for video recordings as another medium to make your lecture an enjoyable experience for your audience. If the technology is not available to use PowerPoint or videos, then improvise. You could create handouts for your audience to follow along. In my speech communication class, I have students use fill-in-the-blank handouts. As I lecture, they fill in the blanks with key concept terms and definitions. You can also use flip charts if you do not have a computer and projector. In the end, use what resources and media that you have to make the presentation as interactive as possible.

Develop Activities and Discussions That Involve Your Audience in the Experience

If you are teaching someone to drive a car, write a paper, conceptualize a theory, create an advertisement, take someone's vital signs, or any other skill, idea, or concept, it is important to provide hands-on experiences. Reading and memorizing terms is not enough for the learner to have a complete understanding of the concepts that you teach. When presenting a lecture or conducting a workshop, you must include some type of activity that involves the student in the material. When I taught writing to fifth graders, I gave mini lessons about the concepts. Then they would write and I would edit their work in one-on-one conferences. They would rewrite their essays after our conference. This was a laborious, daily task, but the students learned. Giving handouts where they underline subjects and double underline predicates did not teach effective writing. When teaching theoretical concepts, learners must be engaged in activities if they are to comprehend the concepts. Writing assignments that challenge students to consider the principles to the point that they can write about them is one way to assist them.

There are other methods of involving students in the material during lectures and workshops. Below is a list with examples, and there are books and online sources with a plethora of ideas to assist you in providing your audience with experiences that support your curricula.

> *Class Discussions.* Class discussions can be facilitated with the class as a whole. Think of an open-ended question to ask. The possibilities are endless. Textbooks provide discussion questions that can be used as well. Although I use group and dyad discussions more than class discussions, I ask students to share a time when they were nervous when giving a speech. Some of the stories have been rather entertaining. Then I ask the student who remembers that experience if someone remembers their bad experience. The answer is that they are the only one who remembers and saw that as a moment of weakness. I add stories about when I was nervous. We laugh and then I tell them to forget bad past experiences and move on. I too have been terrified when giving presentations and do not perceive their nervousness as a weakness. This exercise allows them to realize that their experiences can be used as lessons learned in the education process.

> *Group Discussions.* Put students in groups of four or five. Then pose a discussion question and have them share their

experiences or solve a problem within the group. I teach semester classes and put students in groups of four on the first day. I tell them to learn the names and majors of each person in their groups. Afterward, one person in the group introduces all group members to the class. I ask that they remember the people in their groups so when I ask that they get in a group, they can do so quickly. It allows students the opportunity to get to know three other people in the class and assists them in feeling more confident when presenting. One of the other group discussions that I use is for students to conduct mock job interviews. I give students fifteen frequently asked questions during job interviews. They go round robin telling the job that they would like to obtain and then each student is asked one of the questions by the other members in the group. This process is continued until each student has been asked at least three questions. I walk around listening to the discussions. Then I ask each group who they would hire for the job based on the answers provided and why.

Dyad Discussions. Students can be asked simple questions to be discussed with a person nearby. This can be as simple as asking students to explain the concept you just discussed with one other person. You can also ask them to engage in an activity with one other person to emphasize a point. I found such an activity in my speech communication textbook (Devito, 2006).

When I am discussing nonverbal communication we discuss eye contact. To consider the idea of the "right amount" of eye contact I ask students to talk with one other person in the class about any topic. I give suggestions such as what you did last summer, what you want to do when you graduate from college, what is your favorite hobby, but the topic suggestions are designed to encourage dyad communication. While communicating with their partner, learners are asked to consider who is making the most eye contact. Is it the person speaking or the person listening?

Then I ask them to make complete eye contact. Stare at their partner without looking away. After they try that for a few minutes, I ask that they continue the conversation without making any eye contact. They are to look down or away, while continuing the conversation. When the activity is complete, we have a class discussion about who was most uncomfortable with all or none.

Some students prefer the stare down, while others prefer no eye contact. We discuss the differences and appropriateness of the eye contact duration. Dyad groups can be used effectively to simply allow two people to discuss the information or be utilized to more thoroughly discuss or interact about the concept. Either way, it is a valuable tool to involve students in the learning experience.

Online Discussions. Online discussions are frequently used in online course rooms to provide learners a forum to discuss the principles in the course. This tool is also helpful in traditional courses where the technology is available. Online discussions typically ask students to respond to a question and write a reply that would connect a concept learned with an experience that they have had. Questions where the answers would be the same for each student are not helpful with online discussions.

One online discussion that I post to my communication classes is to consider the best communicator that they know. Write at least 150 words describing who the communicator is and what traits he or she has that is effective. What lessons can you learn from this adept communicator? Then students are asked to read all of the responses and reply to co-learners' responses from which they could identify with or that was the most striking. The reply must be at least seventy-five words. My online classes have twenty online discussions. The idea is to ask students to formulate replies and responses that assist them to thoroughly consider the concepts.

Brainstorming Sessions. Another activity that can be facilitated with the class is small groups, or dyad brainstorming sessions. This is when you ask students to brainstorm ways to solve a problem or discuss their understanding of the topic. Again, I use a brainstorming activity that I found in materials from my speech communication course textbook (Devito, 2006). Before I lecture about interpersonal relationships, I ask students to get into groups and brainstorm. They are to write the five characteristics that comprise a healthy relationship, and then write three things that would cause a relationship to deteriorate or dissolve. After they formulate their lists, a member of each group is to come to the whiteboard and write down the good and bad characteristics. Every time I have done this, the answers provided from one group to the next overlap. Answers for good traits traditionally include words like trust, honesty, communication, sense of humor, active listening, commonalities, and respect. The traits that are usually given that will cause a relationship to deteriorate include things like unfaithfulness, dishonesty, abuse, lack of communication, jealousy, and lack of respect. We then discuss how these concepts are the same things that will be discussed in the lecture. Every adult in the class has had a relationship with another person and understands the components of a good relationship. We then discuss how to create and maintain healthy relationships with friends, partners, and coworkers. Brainstorming sessions highlight the knowledge base that the students understand, so you can build upon these ideas.

Role Playing. Role playing incorporates giving students a scenario and asking volunteers to act out how the scene would play out in real life. It is an enjoyable activity, but cannot be used by students who would not be comfortable in performing an impromptu scenario. Ask students before the lecture if they would be comfortable acting out a scenario, or ask for volunteers. I have asked drama students to do this before class, and they are usually thrilled with the activity. My speech majors are quick to volunteer as well. One scenario example could be to ask two students to imagine that they are working together and one begins telling his colleague a negative story about their boss. You know that this person is a gossip and wants to pull you into the conversation. Play out the scenario so that you do not offend your colleague but do not give him a story about you to spread around. Giving learners examples that they may be confronted with is a fantastic way of conceptualizing a concept more thoroughly.

Games. There are various games that you can use to engage your audience. These can be competitive or involve the class as a whole. I have adapted the game, who wants to be a millionaire, to who wants to get an A. For this game, I ask students to answer a question, and the first five people who bring the correct answer to me are the five contestants in the game. Then I call them up one-by-one. They are asked five questions about the concepts that I have taught, and are given multiple choice answers for each question. If they get stumped, they have two call-outs. The contestant can ask one other person in the room for an answer, or they can poll the room for the correct multiple choice answer. If the contestant misses a question, the next person is brought up for a round of questions. If more than one person gets all five questions, the runners up will be asked questions until there is a winner. I have a colleague who has designed a Jeopardy game to prepare students for their exams. You can create crossword puzzles and word searches for key terms. There are additional resources that explain games you can use to reinforce the information you are teaching.

Problem-solving Activities. Problem-solving activities that can be completed in a short period of time could be discussions of how to handle an ethical dilemma. For example, you could ask students to consider ways to talk to an employee who is late for work. You may also ask students how to best approach a boss who has asked her to do something that the student would find unethical. Groups can also be brought together to work on more complex problems.

Collaborative Groups. If you have time to place learners in collaborative groups to solve a problem that they may be faced with in their professional careers, do it. In this situation, it is important that your instructions are clear and that each group member is assigned a role. Groups of four to five function better than larger groups. If you ask a group of people to solve a problem, be specific about the outcomes expected.

One extensive group activity that I have used in class is to ask students to choose five people to layoff out of a list of ten employees. The groups are provided hypothetical work histories and demographics of the ten people who have the same years of experience with the company. Then they develop criteria, brainstorm possibilities, and come to a consensus of who to retain and who to layoff. They present their decisions to the class, who can ask questions about their decisions.

Service-learning Activities. You may want to extend group or individual projects where students complete an activity that will assist an organization or individual within the community. This type of activity provides learners with real-life experiences. For example, one of my colleagues asks collaborative groups to think about a problem that exists in their community or in an individual's life. He asks students to brainstorm a problem that they can change. Then groups are required to volunteer their services to an organization or an individual and then discuss the experience with the class. Groups from his classes have worked at animal shelters, soup kitchens, the Salvation Army, United Way organizations, local schools, and nursing homes. There was one group who went to an elderly woman's home and raked her yard, cooked a meal, and provided her with companionship for an afternoon. I was so inspired by this activity that I used this experience as a collaborative activity in classes.

Team-building Activities. There are many team-building activities that you can find by searching the internet. Icebreakers and team-building activities liven up a lecture or workshop by getting people moving and communicating with each other. When we begin our group projects in my speech communication classes, I bring in five sets of Tinker Toys. The groups are asked to compete and build the tallest structure that can stand on its own in ten minutes. Through this activity they discuss leadership and membership roles in their groups. It is a favorite activity for that class.

In the end, consider activities and discussions that engage learners in the concepts that you discuss. Every lecture or workshop should explain the concepts and involve the audience. This can be accomplished with group discussions, interactive activities, or collaborative learning. Adult learners have experiences and knowledge that can be built upon when introducing new concepts. Activities and discussions allow students to learn from each other.

Employ Immediacy Behaviors

Research suggests that students believe that they learn more from instructors who display immediacy behaviors (McCroskey & Richmond, 1992). Immediacy behaviors include using the student's name, making eye contact, open posture, use of gestures, and smiling. Read the immediacy behavior chapter for a clearer definition of each behavior. These behaviors are thought to enhance learning because students are more motivated and stimulated by teachers who are enthusiastic about the subject area and care about the students. "Hence, immediate teachers arouse students, draw attention to themselves, have that attention directed to the content being taught, and produce more student learning" (McCroskey & Richmond, 1992, p. 111).

If you do not care about students, do not teach. If you are not passionate about your subject area, teach something else. Teachers who care about their students and their subject area can learn to use immediacy behaviors. Because you love your subject area and believe that you are giving students valuable information that will benefit them throughout their lives, the use of immediacy behaviors should come naturally. When you stand to present, have a positive attitude toward your audience. If a person in your audience annoys you, do not let it show. Focus on the rest of the people in your audience. You do need to maintain a sense of control, but make every effort to not appear angry. You maintain the respect and interest of an audience if you appear confident, competent, charismatic, and caring. Dr. Kehoe (2008) explains this concept when describing how an audience understands your level of caring:

> They notice when we make an effort to get off our notes or slides and actually look at them when we talk about something we love. They notice when we adjust our words or repeat ourselves as frowns of uncertainty cloud their faces. They notice when we energize our lectures, structure them well, tell stories, and learn to visually engage them. (Kehoe, 2008, par. 22)

Your audience knows and appreciates it when you make every effort to prepare a meaningful presentation that you share because you care about them learning.

Delivery

If possible, videotape yourself giving a lecture. You will want to use the same delivery techniques as in any other presentation. Vocal variety is important. A mundane presenter will lull an audience into a mentally inert state. Avoid vocalized pauses that are distracting. I have heard twenty-minute presentations that were so full of "ums" that I wanted to run screaming. You may move about or toward your audience, but do not pace. If you sit in a chair, lean forward. Do not read from your notes or face your PowerPoint slides. Talk to your audience. Lectures need to be animated to hold the attention of learners, and free from distractions.

Construct an Effective Close

As with shorter speeches, lectures should have a conclusion. I would put the objectives on the last slide if using a PowerPoint. Remind your audience of the goals of the presentation, which were your objectives. Quickly review the objectives. Reiterate each objective to enhance recall. Before you put up the last slide, let them know if you are going to have an activity or have a question and answer session after you summarize the presentation. Listeners who see a closing slide go up tend to mentally prepare to leave. You will signal your closing statements of your lecture by saying something like, "We are going to review our objectives again so you can remember what you have learned. Afterward, I have an activity."

I have asked students to not start packing up to leave until my time is up. If you have been asked to teach a subject and are given forty-five minutes, go thirty-five to forty minutes. Do not take more time than allotted or you will lose your audience. Also, do not ask someone if you can go over your allotted time. I was in a workshop that was pretty interesting. Then the speaker asked the person organizing the meeting if she could go about five minutes over. You could see the minds of the audience flying out of the building. The organizer is going to say "yes," even if he or she is thinking, "Please, no. These folks won't like you if you keep them over." I found out later that she had not taken all of her time when she asked for more time, but the audience thought that she had, so they mentally went away. If you are going to exceed your allotted time, keep it to yourself, and do not go over by more than a few minutes. After you let your audience know that you are concluding, then do not start down any new paths. The conclusion should be just that; provide a brief summary. Then you would want to open the floor for questions.

Formulate Questions That Engage Learners

Before the lecture, during the lecture, and at the end of the lecture are all good times to ask discussion question. You can ask questions such as, "Who remembers the seven elements of communication from our last session?" Then you will need to allow your audience to refer to notes so they can read back a response, but this will not fully engage learners in the content. If you begin your presentation with a discussion, ask students to relate information that they already know about the subject area. You may also want to ask them about an experience that they have had with the topic during the lecture. For example, if you were going to teach students how to present a motivational speech, you could ask them to think about a motivational speech and what made the speech inspirational. Write the traits of a good motivational speaker on the board as the students share the characteristics. This technique includes asking students to tell a story when they have had an experience with the topic.

For instance, if you were teaching an audience about the need for good customer service within a company, you could ask people to share a story about when they received terrible customer service from another organization. Then ask the audience to tell about a time when they received excellent customer service. Beginning your lecture with discussion questions focuses the audience on your topic.

Throughout the lecture, you can open the floor for discussions, or put students in buzz groups for a few minutes. "Buzz groups are usually made up of three or four students who are given a few minutes once or twice during a lecture to discuss a question or an issue that arises" (Brookfield & Preskill, 2005, p.47). During buzz groups, ask each student to share feelings about the topic area. Classroom discussions in the lecture could be asking a student to relate an experience about the subject. I discuss the scripts that we write that are full of social norms. As a class, we go through the restaurant script. They explain what we do from the time that we walk in the door of a local restaurant, to the time that we pay the bill.

> We enter the restaurant, a host or hostess asks how many are in our party. We walk to the table. A server asks what we would like to drink and if we would like an appetizer. We are then asked what we would like to order for our entrée. Food is brought to the table and drinks are filled. Then we are asked if we would like dessert. Finally, we call the server to give us our bill. We leave the amount on the check along with a tip.

I explain that the script changes if we go to Europe where a host or hostess is not waiting for us at the door and a drink such as water is a bottle of water that is not refilled. This gets my point across while involving them in the lecture. Think of questions that would involve your audience throughout the lecture.

Final Questions

After the lecture is over, encourage questions. If you want everyone to participate in asking questions, you may want to have them write the questions or concerns, so you can address the questions the next time you meet. If you will not be meeting with this audience again, you can e-mail answers to everyone soon after the presentation. You would also want to ask a few people to ask their questions or share comments after they have written their questions. Below is a list of questions you could ask students to answer orally or in writing to provide feedback. The questions below have been adapted from Stephen Brookfield and Stephen Preskill's (2005) book, *Discussion as a way of teaching: Tools and techniques for democratic classrooms*.

1. What questions have gone unanswered about today's topic?
2. What point or concept that was discussed did you find most interesting or useful?
3. What point or concept was least interesting or useful?
4. What point or concept did you find the most confusing?
5. During the lecture, when were you most engaged as a learner?

This list of questions also serves as an evaluation of your presentation. If you give this to students as a questionnaire, it would be best to make them anonymous.

Summary

This chapter explained how to conduct interactive lectures or workshops. Realize that adults learn by building on their present knowledge, and they want to know how the information you teach relates to them. Present information with clarity and incorporate resources to provide credibility. While designing your lecture, provide visual images such as PowerPoint or Prezi presentations, pictures, models, diagrams, graphs, and videos. Involve your audience in the learning experience using activities and discussion questions. Visuals, activities, and discussions that assist people of the three most recognized learning styles: visual, auditory, and kinesthetic. Anytime that you are presenting, use immediacy behaviors. Conclude with a summary. If possible, allow time for final questions or give students anonymous questionnaires. These questionnaires can also provide the speaker with feedback.

Evaluation for Lecture

Introduction   **Comments**

Explain need to learn topic   _____

Present three to six objectives   _____

Objectives use Bloom's
Taxonomy   _____

Body

Points clear   _____

Incorporate resources or research   _____

Back up information with
personal story   _____

Support points with examples   _____

Used figurative language   _____

Language appropriate   _____

Completed in time frames   _____

Conclusion

Signal that you are concluding   _____

Summarized objectives   _____

Used activity or discussions to
involve audience   _____

Provide a creative and
meaningful close   _____

Final question/answer session
engage audience   _____

Delivery

Eye contact   _____

Vocal variety   _____

Friendly and enthusiastic   _____

Natural gestures   _____

Personable language   _____

Total   _____

Evaluation for PowerPoint Presentation

Comments

Objectives   _____

Importance of the topic   _____

Main points   _____

Supporting data   _____

Resource data   _____

Images or pictures   _____

Six-point rule   _____

Animation   _____

Aesthetics   _____

Conclusion   _____

Total   _____

References

Brookfield, S. D. & Preskill, S. (2005). *Discussions as a way of teaching: Tools and techniques for democratic classrooms*. San Francisco, CA: Jossey-Bass.

DeVito, Joseph (2006) *Human Communication: The Basic Course*, 11th ed. Allyn & Bacon/Longman.

Griffin, Em. (1997). *A first look at communication theory 3rd ed.* McGraw-Hill.

Kehoe, D. (2008, Dec. 1). Five ways to energize your lectures. *UA/AU University Affairs*. Retrieved from http://www.universityaffairs.ca/five- ways-to-energize-your-lectures.aspx

Kelly, M. (2010). *Learning styles: Understanding and using learning styles*. Retrieved from http://712educators.about.com/od/learning styles/a/ learning_styles.htm

Lutz, W. (1990). *Double-Speak*. New York: Harper Perennial.

McCroskey, J. & Richmond, V. (1992). Power in the classroom: Communication, control, and concern. Hillsdale, New Jersey. Lawrence Erlbaum Associates.

Overbaugh, R. C. & Schultz, L. (n. d.). *Bloom's Taxonomy*. Retrieved from   http://www.odu.edu/educ/roverbau/Bloom/blooms_ taxonomy.htm

Tennant, M. & Pogson, P. (1995). *Learning and change in the adult years: A developmental perspective*. San Francisco, CA: Jossey-Bass.

Chapter Nine

Impromptu Speeches

The objectives of this chapter are to:

✓ Define impromptu speeches.
✓ Understand how to organize the impromptu speech.
✓ Examine rules for impromptu speeches.
✓ Answer questions effectively.
✓ Demonstrate a confident and friendly posture.
✓ Answer media interview questions.
✓ Avoid errors during impromptu speeches.

Extemporaneous speeches are prepared and practiced and few notes are used. Impromptu speeches are given with little to no preparation time. These are actually the everyday speeches that you should always be prepared to present. Impromptu speeches are given by professionals and even in personal situations. This chapter will assist you in being prepared when you are not given any time to prepare. Below are examples of impromptu presentations.

> *Business meeting.* You are at a business meeting and your boss asks you to give a brief report concerning the project that you are working on or you are asked to give a summary about the conference you attended. The company or organization is investing in you, your project, and conferences you attend. It is important that you confidently present information and yourself to the group.

> *Accept an award.* You are in the back of the room for the quarterly regional meeting and are thinking about the to-do list on your desk. Then you hear your name. Snapping back to reality, your boss says, "Come on up here and say a few words." Everyone in the room begins applauding, and you realize that you won the employee of the quarter award. You need to look like the star employee of the quarter.

> *Media interview.* The local television station called your office and asks for an interview. Ten minutes prior, you discovered that one of your delivery vans was involved in an

accident and your employee, along with two other people, were transported to the hospital.

Job interview. You went to the job interview. You prepared and practiced the most asked interview questions, but the interview committee is asking questions that do not relate to the job or what you have practiced. It is not the time to panic.

"Say a few words" moments. You are at fund raising event for your favorite nonprofit organization. The coordinator of the event says, "Please say a few words of inspiration to our volunteers and donors."

Question and answer sessions after a presentation are mini impromptu speeches. Although you prepared for the presentation, you do not want to lose credibility during this portion of the presentation.

Everyday Speeches

When you go to meetings and conferences, you should be prepared, just in case you are called upon to present. Those who have a reputation for being talented speakers may be called upon if a planned public speaker does not show. If you have a talent for speaking, prepare a speech in an area that you are an expert (King). Do not be obnoxious and speak at every meeting you attend. But if you are asked to fill in for another speaker, be ready and willing. Perhaps, you have already given a presentation that is similar to what you are being asked to present. Use portions of previous presentations. To gain experience in giving extemporaneous and impromptu speeches, join a Toastmasters Club.

If you are asked to say a few words at a meeting at work, a ceremony, or a family event, briefly share with your audience. Again, you do not want to be the obnoxious person who drones on and on at events, but there are many opportunities where you should give brief speeches. For example, if you are giving someone a shower, birthday party, congratulatory party, reception, or are presenting an award to the employee of the day, you should give a brief presentation commemorating the person that you have come together to celebrate. If an award is worth giving, it is worth formally presenting it to the recipient. A brief presentation that highlights the person makes the commemorative event more meaningful.

Think Organization

You should have enough experience with presentations that you can quickly organize an impromptu speech. Think of the impromptu speech as a two-minute informative or motivational speech. The organization is the same but condensed. You will have an introduction, body, and conclusion. You can use topical organization where you make one or two points, support the points with examples, anecdotes, and/or supporting data. If the speech is to be persuasive, you would probably use problem solution order. For example, if you are asked to persuade or inspire an audience at a charity fundraiser, think about the purpose of the organization. What is the problem that the organization is trying to solve? Mention that problem and then state that the solution is why you are there. Back it up with a specific testimony of how someone was helped by the work of donors and volunteers. Do not ramble on. If you have five minutes to prepare, write the main points that you will make and be organized.

Introductions

If you are given a few minutes to consider an attention grabber such as a story, quote, current event, statistic, or startling action, start with an attention grabber. If nothing comes to mind, simply restate the question. Then as a preview to the body of the speech, tell your audience the point that you would like to make. For example, if you are asked to discuss the project you are working on, stand with confidence. It is okay to give a minute pause as you collect your thoughts. You can begin by enthusiastically saying something like, "I appreciate the opportunity to discuss my team's project. One of the parts of the project is to improve communication concerning our products and services to target audiences. A simple idea that we will implement is to advertise on Web sites that are preferred by our target audience." You have given a brief overview of what your team is working on and one area of concentration. Now you are ready to explain your points.

Getting to the Point

After your introduction and the preview, you will explain a point or two and then support it. Do not veer off into other points or random thoughts. This is not the time to go into the four months of research or a detailed account of the topic. Get to the point. Consider supporting data such as an explanation, statistic, illustration, or story. To continue the example above, you could provide a statistic and hypothetical situation. "Our marketing team has projected that the cost of Internet advertisements will be less expensive than advertisements in local newspapers. Such advertisements will focus on our customer base. We anticipate that this change will not only lower advertisement costs, but also increase sales by 7 percent over the coming year." You may have another point and bring in an example about how a competitor had similar results. Then go to the conclusion.

Final Summary

You do need to provide closure to every speech by giving a final summary. A conclusion signal will assist your audience in understanding that you are almost finished talking. Then summarize, and you can even encourage questions. For example, "In the end, I am proud of my team for their hard work. It is a pleasure to have the opportunity to give you this very brief example of one of the accomplishments we have made so far. We are moving into the implementation stages of advertising our products and services to the markets that will enhance growth. If you have any questions, please do not hesitate to let me know." Now, smile, pause, and sit down. Once you have wowed them with an organized, informative presentation, it is time to let the meeting proceed.

Brevity Is Essential

Although brevity has been mentioned throughout, it is essential to the impromptu speech. I am sure that you can remember times when someone was asked to "say a few words" and the speaker rambled on and on. If you are asked to speak for a few minutes, that is a time frame. When I am nervous, I tend to talk too much. If you are at a ceremony, business meeting, or celebratory event, you do not want to dominate the time. It will cause you to lose credibility with your audience. A group appreciates important information that is shared without wasting their time. It is not the time to show the audience how intelligent you are. The impromptu speaker who speaks with brevity will be asked to speak again. George L. Grice and John F. Skinner (2007) suggest a speech axiom or a known principle about public speech, "Stand up! Speak up! Shut up!" This concept should be adhered to when giving an impromptu speech.

Answering Questions

Question and answer sessions are really impromptu speaking opportunities. After you present a lecture or speech, you may want to allow time for questions from the audience. You may also have a need to answer questions when applying for a scholarship, applying for a promotion, or conducting a media conference. Job interviews are also impromptu in nature. You cannot prepare for every question and backup question, but you can prepare yourself to give concise answers that have a point and support your point with examples.

When answering questions to a group of people, such as in a media conference, attentively listen to the person asking the question. If you do not understand the question, ask the questioner to repeat the question. If there is a word or phrase that you do not understand, say something like, "I am not sure that I understand the question. Would you please rephrase it?" Repeat the question if you understand it but the rest of the audience may not have heard the question. Then pause for just a moment. Answer by talking to everyone in the room, rather than looking only at the person who asked the question. The answer is information that you want to share with the audience, not one individual. Answer the question as concisely as possible, but answer the question. If you do not know, do not try to make something up. If you do not know, you may want to say something like, "That is a great question. I do not have the data in front of me, but I will look that up right away and call you with a response." Make a point to get the person's card if you do not know the questioner and get back with anyone who wants an answer.

There are times that you may be in a question and answer session with a person or persons who are angry. Dealing with an irate questioner should be handled with diplomacy and dignity. First, realize that the people who are angry believe that their anger is justified. Never be disrespectful to an audience member, even if you disagree with his or her point of view. When anger is present, listening is not. Furthermore, when you are the speaker, you are the target. Your audience has something in common. If you insult someone in your audience, everyone may feel vulnerable to an attack. Think about a time when someone in a class that you took was insulted by the instructor. The students in the class probably bonded because they had a common enemy. So what do you do if you have a hostile audience member?

First, stay calm. Do not fire back. Let the person vent and ask the question. Then answer the question with a show of concern. You may even want to answer the next question by this person. If the angry audience member persists and wants to dominate the question/answer session, say something like, "I appreciate your passion for this topic that is so important to me as well. I do not feel that I can adequately answer all of your concerns, now; however, I will meet with you one-on-one right after I have concluded this question and answer session. Right now, allow me to answer some of the concerns from others." Then take a question from someone else. The key is to be respectful but not allow a heckler to control the question and answer session. Answer sympathetically and honestly, but you must maintain control. Allowing an angry audience member to control your emotions in front of others is a mistake.

Anytime that you are speaking to an audience, be cautious. "Remember that in a public gathering there is no such thing as an off-the-record statement" (Grice & Skinner, 2007, p. 382). Jokes, off-color remarks, or an insult to anyone is inappropriate. Listen to the questioner, direct answers to the audience, and ask the questioner if you answered the question to his or her satisfaction. If the questioner is hostile, then refer to the previous example so you can move forward.

Confident yet Friendly Posture

No matter how much you are taken off guard when asked to give an impromptu speech, appear as confident as possible. It may be disconcerting for you to be placed center stage without notice, but be graceful and appear ready. Again, give yourself a few moments to collect your thoughts and composure; then stand up ready to present a concise, well structured presentation. Do not fret. It will be over soon. Maintain a friendly and open posture, remembering concepts of delivery, such as: eye contact, vocal variety, natural gestures, and the omission of vocalized pauses. Silent pauses between points and when you want your audience to ponder a point is acceptable. Delivery should come across as natural, conversational and professional. Showing enthusiasm when appropriate can liven up your brief presentation.

One component to enhance confidence is practice with impromptu speeches. In my public speaking courses, I give students impromptu speech topics to practice. Although the first one or two practice runs are often nerve-wracking, it is a joy to watch the confidence levels go up as they go through the exercise. Table topics in my Toastmasters International Club meetings is a favorite for club members. I would encourage any professional to join a club or to practice impromptu speeches in nonthreatening situations to prepare and to increase confidence.

Media Interviews

Oftentimes, professionals find themselves in a position that they are called upon for an interview with the news media. Media interviews involve talking to a reporter in a one-on-one interview or to a group of reporters. If you are in a profession such as being a public servant or you work in public relations, you should invest in media relations training. If you are called upon to conduct an interview with the media, do not turn them away. President Bill Clinton said, "Never pick a fight with people who buy ink by the barrel." However, if you are asked to talk to a reporter, you can prepare. Ask the reporter questions about the interview. You may say something like, "Tell me how I can assist you in the interview. Is there any specific information that you would like me to gather before you arrive?" If you know about the subject area, jot down main points that you want the media groups' audience to know. Gather any information that will assist the reporter in understanding background knowledge. Your interview may last for fifteen to thirty minutes, but the reporter is looking for sound bites. Your quote in the paper or on the nightly news may consist of one or two sentences. Answer the questions in sound bites and continually mention the main points or speaking points that you would like your audience to know.

Set up the interview in an area that is quiet and free from distractions or confidential material. Make eye contact with the reporter, not the camera, but make eye contact. Do not read responses or look down or away when talking. Gestures should be minimal and keep your hands above your lap or rested on your desk or table. Listen to the question and answer briefly and honestly. If there is another person in your company or organization that knows about the subject area to be discussed, call that person in to the interview. If you have a public relations representative, call that person to come into the interview as well.

If the topic of interest is positive, then be positive and share how thrilled your organization is to help your community. At this point, you can share your company's mission statement or vision statement for free! If the event is negative, then you must be calm, honest, and friendly. As in the example at the beginning of the chapter that a delivery van was involved in an accident, be honest but do not admit guilt. State the facts that you know, but do not suggest that your employee was to blame. Also, do not give names of anyone until you have been approved to do so. Answer the questions and let the interviewer know that you will let him or her know any information that you can confirm as it becomes available. If you are pressed to answer questions that you have not been approved to release, reiterate the fact that you do not have the information but will release it when available.

Although you may be nervous during a media interview, this will not show unless you make such a declaration. Concentrate on the questions and your key points. Avoid mentioning any names or making negative statements. It is also important that your facial movements and vocal variety match your statements. If something tragic has happened, look somber and let your audience know that your heart goes out to the victims. The worst interview that I have seen is when a speaker nervously giggled when telling that someone was hurt. If the interview is about something that is positive, smile. If it is a somber event, look the part. Smiling is a good idea when appropriate. Use open posture, and call the reporter by name during any media interview.

Every organization, company, or corporation should be prepared for media interviews and especially for any crisis that may occur. I have conducted workshops on this topic and believe that preparation beforehand is key in emerging from a crisis while maintaining a positive image with the general public. If you are interviewed by a reporter, be professional, honest, and give concise answers that relay the points that will assist the reporter, your organization, and the audience.

Errors to Avoid

Leon Fletcher (1983) gives four common errors when presenting an impromptu speech: rambling, getting off subject, apologizing, and acting surprised (pp. 132–134). Organize your speech and your thoughts with an introduction, statement of your main points, supporting materials, and a summary. Do not ramble with additional points and ideas. Avoid the temptation to move to another subject. Answer the question or address the topic you have been asked to talk about. Finally, never, ever, apologize or self criticize during any presentation. If you are asked to give an impromptu speech, the audience knows that you have not had time to prepare. Do not state the obvious. Instead, tell the audience that you are honored to share about this topic that you are enthusiastic about. You may be surprised to be called upon to give an impromptu speech, but do not make such statements to your audience. You are a professional and an adept speaker. Walk into any speaking situation with confidence that you can tell your audience what you will discuss, bring up main points, support those points with examples, and summarize what you have already said.

Summary

Speech courses are designed to teach students to choose topics, write outlines, and present informative and persuasion speeches; however, adults are called upon to present themselves without the luxury of preparation. This chapter was designed to assist learners in presenting themselves in classrooms, social settings, and business situations where they do not have time to plan ahead. Topics included types of impromptu speeches, how to quickly organize thoughts with

226 LivingstonRuthLivingston, PhD

an introduction, body, and conclusion, and presentation techniques. Examples were provided. You will be given the opportunity to present impromptu speeches in class, but if I give you the examples in the text it would not be impromptu. So listen to the question, organize your thoughts, think about an introduction, main point(s), example(s), and a summary for the presentation. Be brief, concise, friendly, and confident.

References

Fletcher, L. (1983). *How to speak like a pro.* New York: Ballantine Books.

Grice, G. L. & Skinner, J. F. (2007). *Mastering public speaking 6th ed.* Boston: Pearson.

King, C. (n. d.). *How to give a successful impromptu speech.* Retrieved from http://www.creativekeys.net/PowerfulPresentations/article1015.html

Chapter Ten

Sales Presentations

The objectives of this chapter are to:

- ✓ Define sales presentations.
- ✓ Research product, potential clients, and competitors.
- ✓ Listen to potential clients.
- ✓ Ask situational questions.
- ✓ Prepare for objections.
- ✓ Understand prospect's needs.
- ✓ Organize sales presentations.
- ✓ Utilize time effectively.
- ✓ Prepare an interactive presentation.

Professional presentations, like a workshop, motivational speech, board meeting reports, job interviews, or media interviews, are mostly persuasive presentations. Successful professionals consistently sell a product, company, and self. Speak with confidence and knowledge about your product or service, client need, and value of your product or service. Individuals who speak negatively about their organization take away from their product, company, or self-image. Consider yourself an ambassador for your organization.

A successful sales presentation requires extensive preparation, analysis, research, and practice. It requires an accumulation of the skills discussed in this book. You must understand the basics of presentations based upon Aristotle's principles. Delivery techniques will include the use of immediacy behaviors to enhance the credibility and likeability of the presenter. The sales presentation must be motivational to move an audience to buy your product or service. Listening and interviewing are imperative to understanding the needs of the client. The sales presentation, as a lecture or workshop, will begin with you establishing objectives or goals for the presentation. Your information must be presented clearly and concisely. Be prepared to answer any questions that may come your way. If you are called upon to represent your business or organization, you should train and practice to become a winner in sales that will rival all competitors. This chapter provides tips for creating a winning sales presentation. It begins with learning about the product or service that you are selling and learning about potential clients and competitors. The presentation is tailored to meet the needs of the potential client. Clearly explain the product and how purchasing your product or service will grow the company's profits or bottom line. Then go for the close.

Know All There Is to Know

If you are going to sell a product or service, you need to know everything you can learn about the product or service. What are the advantages? How do your costs match up to the competition? Are there any weaknesses? You also need to know the history of your organization. It is not necessary that your presentation explain all of the advantages, but you should know how what you are selling will meet the needs of every possible client. If you are selling insurance, for example, you would want to understand the advantages of different insurance products for people of various ages and life situations. You are the expert about the products and should speak with authority about every facet of your product or service. Knowledge gives you the power to pick and choose the information that would be of interest to different people, businesses, or organizations.

Put information about the product in an information packet. Brochures, fact sheets, and annual reports should be created to add to the packets. Brochures can be created that are specific to a variety of target audiences. Every item that you provide your prospective clients should look professional. If the media has written positive articles about your product or organization, place the articles in your packet. You can volunteer to write an informative article about your area of expertise for a business journal or news outlet. Be recognized as the expert.

Believe in Your Product or Service

For you to persuade others, you must be in compliance. If an insurance salesperson wants you to buy a life insurance policy, ask to see her policy. I worked for an insurance agent for five years and consulted with clients about insurance needs. I sold life insurance policies that I believed would be a great benefit to our clients. I still have the policies that I bought then, and only advised people to purchase the insurance that would meet their needs. Sometimes I advised policy holders to cancel a specific coverage that was not necessary. My belief in the products and concern for clients built a bond of trust.

Belief in your product or service is essential to sales. Salesman Billy Cox said, "Selling is only a transfer of belief; it's simply helping others believe the same way you believe about a product or service" (Cox, par. 1).

Your belief will show in your words and body language. Clients can intuitively read your body language if you have a passion for your product. If you are not sold on your product or service or do not believe in your organization, I would suggest finding a career at a company that you are proud to be a part.

Research Your Potential Client's Company or Organization

After you have learned all that you can about your product or service and your organization, extensively research your potential clients. Find out all that you can about a target area and identify companies or organizations in that area that have a need for your product. If you want to sell a product to hotels in the area, you should research how many hotels are in the area and how many need your product. Conduct a market analysis. You may need to encourage your company or organization to hire an analyst if you or someone in your organization does not have the expertise to conduct a market analysis. This will assist you in identifying potential clients. After you identify your most promising target market, list the specific individuals that you need to contact. If it is your job to set up appointments for your sales presentations, read books about how to obtain new clients and even go to seminars to learn the art. Two books that deal with the topic are *Selling to VITO: The very important top officer* by Anthony Parinello (1999), and *Get clients now* by C. J. Hayden (2007). There are other books that give unique ideas to arranging the presentation.

Before you give a sales presentation to an organization, know the history of the organization, the hierarchical structure or who makes the decisions to buy, and find the projections of what you can do to help their bottom line. Read everything that you can find on the Internet about the organization. If the company has a Web site, you should read all of it. Read local and corporate Web sites. Write the mission and vision statements. Review strategic plans and annual reports. Search for advertisements. You should also go to the organization or industry and talk to people. Watch the operations of the business or industry so you get a sense of the corporate culture. This information will help you to tailor your presentation to meet the needs of a specific audience.

Listen to Your Potential Client

To learn about potential client needs, you must be a good listener. Aldo Zini suggests that the first meeting with potential clients should not be a discussion about your product or service but a time of listening to the potential client. "Your first sales call should be just to go in and ask questions and see if they're a good fit for the product" (Zini, 2009, p. 2). Discovering the compatibility of your product and customer need will save time and will assist you in designing an effective presentation. Ask questions and take copious notes. You should have researched the strategic plan and mission. Now find out which objective in the plan is being implemented. Ask about the goals and needs of the organization. Ask about current priorities.

Listening also builds trust, the foundation to persuasion. Attentive listening shows clients that you are concerned about their needs. Listen empathically, working to consider the clients' perspectives. Once you have asked a question, allow the interviewee to thoughtfully consider the answers. Never, ever interrupt. The impressions that you make will have a great deal to do with you making the sale. Overly aggressive salespeople do not make a good impression. Actively listen. Maintain an open posture, ask clarifying questions, and remain positive. Read the listening chapter in this text for instruction for improving listening skills.

Research Your Competitors' Strengths and Weaknesses

Research your competitors by asking people who have used your competitors the strengths and weaknesses of the competition. If you know what others like about the competition, you can simulate those qualities. The weaknesses can be avoided once discovered (Hayden, 2007). You should search the web to learn about the competitor's products, services, and history. Find advertisements of competitors. Ascertain the cost differences and the product differences. How can your product or service better meet the needs of the client than the competitor's product or service? If you cannot discover benefits due to cost and quality, then your organization needs to make improvements to remain competitive. You are selling your brand and image. Know what gives your brand a competitive edge.

Ask Your Client Situational Questions about the Presentation

If you are going to give any presentation, you need to ask questions about the location, technology, time frames, and the number of people who will attend. The room needs to be comfortable and well lit. If you are presenting to a few people in a large room, move the audience close to you. Presentational aids such as PowerPoint presentations should be shown without the need to turn off lights. Only use visual aids that will benefit your presentation. Remember that the sales presentation is a persuasive speech. If you focus too much on presentation aids, it can distract the listener. If you will give a sales presentation more than once, you should have professional presentation posters made that can be easily displayed. These posters could include important data graphically displayed. If you have presentation aids that include audio, be sure that the equipment is operational. Always arrive early and test equipment. Have a backup plan if the equipment is not working or if the projector is not of the quality that you can leave the lights on when you present.

It is important that you ask about time frames and stay within time frames. In fact, you should complete your presentation before the time that you have been given has elapsed. If you have only been given ten minutes, pack a punch in six minutes. The moment your time is up, people will mentally leave your presentation, anyway. Ask about the number of people so you can prepare handouts for everyone, and provide the participants with a business card.

If you are setting up the room for your presentation, make it as cozy as possible. Rid the room of clutter and noise. You should also provide refreshments (Parinello, 1999). Practice the presentation in the room with the equipment. The room where you present should look professional and be well lit. It is best to have presentation aids already set up so you are not fumbling with flip charts or computers. If the presentation is ten minutes or less, it might be best to use fewer presentation aids. Graphical posters are most helpful if you do not have the time or equipment for visual aids that require technology. A two-minute, professionally edited video can add to shorter presentations if the equipment is available. If you are presenting to only one person, you might be able to use your laptop. You will need plenty of practice if using a laptop for a presentation, but it is possible with a brief presentation for one to three people. Do not bog your audience down with information overload.

Prepare Yourself for Objections

You should prepare for any questions that may appear negative and for being turned down. The Internet site Changing Minds.org provides a process for and techniques to deal with objections called LACE. First, *listen* to the objections so you can fully understand. Ask questions and if there are any other objections. Secondly, *accept* the objections. Do not react negatively. Instead consider the objection from the potential client's point of view. Third, make a *commitment* to address their objections if they will commit to purchase your product or service. Finally, take *explicit* action. Either assist him or her to reframe the objection or to rephrase the objection in a more positive way. If this is not possible, it may be time to negotiate terms (ChangingMinds.org).

A friend of mine, Lee Boyd, suggested that a "P" for preparation should be added to LACE. Before the presentation, one must prepare. Consider the objections that may arise and consider the best way to handle each. Research possible answers that you can give that are positive and effective. Do not argue or downplay the objections. The potential clients should be treated with respect at all times. If you become defensive or argumentative, you will lose the prospect. By actively listening to the objection, you can learn the concerns of the client. If you downplay the objection or try to make a client feel ridiculous, the client will become defensive and think of even more reasons not to buy.

Think about a time that you raised an objection in a conversation. If the person you were speaking with made any attempt to make you feel like your point of view did not have merit, you probably became defensive and angry. Let the client know that you understand the concern. You may want to consider examples about how a client had a similar concern and how those concerns were dealt with. Then tell the happy ending about how the product or service helped that client achieve his or her goals. Randy Pausch discussed the positives of obstacles in his motivational presentation "The Last Lecture."

Brick walls are there for a reason. The brick walls are not there to keep us out. The brick walls are there to show how badly we want something because the brick walls are there to stop the people who don't want something badly enough. They are there to keep out the other people.

Anything worth striving for will be difficult. If you are easily discouraged, you will not succeed in persuading others. If you believe in yourself and that your product will help your clients, you will find a way over the wall.

Prepare Your Presentation Equipped with the Knowledge of Your Prospect's Needs

A persuasive presentation begins with an attention grabber, establishes credibility, previews the speech, and then identifies a need. You should know the needs of your prospective client and convince the decision makers within the company that your product or service will meet or satisfy the need. Prepare a presentation that meets the unique needs of the potential client. Consider the current priorities of the organization and the overall goal and mission of the company. If you can identify how buying what you are selling will increase their bottom line, you can make the sale.

Get to the point. Identify the need that they have and how your product or service will help them solve the need. Show projections about how this purchase will help them meet their goals. Help the decision makers visualize their company growth if they buy your product or service. People you persuade must understand how you are helping them, all the while being convinced that you have their best interests at heart.

Organizing Your Presentation

It is important that your presentation is well organized. Below is a way to organize a sales presentation. At the end of the chapter a worksheet to prepare for the presentation and template outline is provided.

Grab your Audience's Attention. As with any speech you will ever present, the first statement out of your mouth should be an attention grabber. The attention grabber relates to your topic and is used to captivate your audience so they will focus and intently listen. Techniques include a dramatic story, asking a question, mentioning a current event, a startling phrase or action, a startling statistic, arousing curiosity, reciting a powerful quote, or using humor. Do not start with a joke unless it relates, and it is definitely funny. Consider using more than one technique if your idea will reach out and capture your audience's focus. You stand with as much confidence as you can manage, smile at the people to whom you are presenting. Have your attention grabber memorized so you do not need to read anything in those first moments of your presentation. If you are telling a story, make it vivid and powerful. If you are asking a question, make it meaningful. The first moments of your presentation can either draw your audience to you or move them away. It is important that you do not use any offensive language at any time; starting with a word of profanity may startle your audience but not in a positive way.

Introduce Your Company and your Presentation Team. Give a brief introduction of everyone who will be presenting. Do not wait to make introductions until it is time for each person to speak. You should tell why the members of the team are qualified to present. Then you should give a brief overview of your organization. Create the introductions of presenters and the company as a way to provide credibility. This portion is important, but be brief.

Transition to the Body. Before you begin the body of the presentation, give the audience a preview of what you will discuss. Let the listeners know that during the presentation, you will clearly and briefly describe your product or service and the benefits to the client's company. Then you will tell them the full costs and how this will increase the client's growth potential. Let them know the goals of the presentation.

Clearly Explain Your Product or Service. You should explain what your product or service is. Be clear but avoid being technical, and do not use jargon. Make this informative portion of the presentation as interactive as possible. This would be the worst time to bore your audience. You should provide samples of the goods or services if possible. If you have a consulting business, explain the expertise you provide and you may want to give a brief demonstration. Involve audience members if possible. In other words, put your product in the hands of the audience. Give them a taste of your product or service.

Explain how Your Product or Service will Assist the Prospect in Reaching Company Goals. You need to make a case for how what you are offering meets the specific needs of the organization. You must have an understanding of the goals, missions, and current priorities to convincingly establish the idea that your product or service will assist the organization. If your product or service will not assist them in meeting their needs, you should not waste your time on this sales presentation. Vividly, describe the benefits of your product or service. Then explain how their company will improve if they buy your goods or services. The visualization step should be as powerful as possible. Give examples of how other organizations that have used your product or service flourished. If you could show valid growth projections, you will dramatically improve your chances of obtaining the sale.

Give Details about the Costs. You should explain the costs of the product or service, but explain the costs in relationship to benefits. If your prices are better or at least comparable to those of your competitors, reveal this information. If your costs are more than your competitors, explain why your product is of greater value. Be specific about how your organization's products or services are a fit for the prospect. Create a visual of the cost and benefits. This should be an easy to read graphic. Do not inflate the benefits or hide any costs. If your costs are not competitive, you need to adjust the costs before trying to make the sale.

The Conclusion. Signal that you are wrapping up the presentation. This would be a statement as, "In conclusion" or "Let me conclude with a summary of the benefits and the value of our product." Then briefly summarize the need, satisfaction, cost, and bottom line benefits. The ending portion of the presentation should be as powerful as your attention grabber. You could refer back to the attention grabber or tell another story or quote. Let the audience know that you are wrapping up. Then briefly summarize and end with a powerful quote or story. Do not throw out new information such as statistics. The conclusion is a wrap-up, not time to make new points that should have been in the body of the presentation.

The Close. After your impressive presentation, you should seal the deal. Have a contract ready. If they are not ready to buy, ask about the objections and begin negotiations. Ask for questions and concerns. Ask if the client needs information that would help in the decision-making process. You may also ask for another meeting. Do not end the meeting without asking directly if the client is ready to deal. Be prepared for a positive or negative response. C. J. Hayden (2007) suggests answers to common objections during the close of the sales presentation in her book, *Get clients now!* (p. 225).

The prospect says . . .	*You respond . . .*
We can't afford to spend that much.	Yes, I know the price is significant. Let me ask you, what is it costing you not to fix it?
I need to think about it.	It's a big decision, and I'm sure you do. Tell me, what are some of your concerns?
I'm not sure it will help.	Yes, I understand you can't know that until we get started. If it did help, what might you get out of it?
We're too busy right now.	I know how busy you are. Tell me, if you don't deal with the situation now, when will you be less busy?
It's too expensive.	Yes, it's a big investment. What results would make that kind of investment worthwhile?
We're not ready.	I understand that you have a lot going on. What will need to change in order for you to be ready?
I'm not sure you're right for the job.	Yes, I know that you may have concerns about that. What would you need to feel confident about in order to hire me?

Be prepared for a yes or for objections. If you cannot seal the deal just after your presentation, set up a follow-up appointment. If the client is not at all interested, ask if they know of another company or organization that would benefit from your service or product. Also, find out what went wrong with the presentation. What could be done to make the product or service more appealing? Use every opportunity to make the most of this time.

Do Not Waste Time

If you are given the opportunity to speak with the decision makers of an organization, use their time wisely. Consider how to make your presentation as brief and effective as possibly possible. Prepare presentations of varying lengths. You should have a two-minute overview that would get you in for a ten-minute appointment. The sales presentation should be unique to each potential client or target audience. Cut out any information that is not relevant to this specific audience. Explain the product, benefits, costs, and how to sign up. You introduce yourself and your company, but that is not the focus. You are persuading this audience that you have something that will benefit them or help them in reaching their goals. Speak long enough to give substantive information that will assist the listeners in making a decision. Nonetheless, too much information about anything else will be a waste of their time. Eyes will glaze over, watches will be observed, and irritation levels will rise.

Make the Presentation Enjoyable and Interactive

You want to pull your audience in so that they are not wondering when you are going to be quiet and let them get back to work. Imagine the amount of time that these individuals spend listening to others. Organizations will have meetings to discuss upcoming meetings. A meeting with you should be the highlight of their meeting time. Think of a way to make the presentation enjoyable and interactive. Below is a list of delivery techniques that are necessary to maintaining the attention of your audience.

> *Eye contact.* Your presentation should be conversational. If you read more than a line or two of your presentation, the audience's mind will go back to their to-do lists. Maintain eye contact with every individual as you would in a conversation among friends.

> *Vocal variety.* Monotone voices tend to have two outcomes: putting an audience to sleep or annoying them to the point

of no listening capability. Use your voice to set the mood. Be enthusiastic and dramatic.

Smile. Being friendly at all times is essential during a presentation. If you are talking about something sad, you would not smile. But maintain a friendly demeanor.

Open posture. Of course, maintain an open posture. If someone mentions objections or has a negative comment, continue to maintain an open posture. Do not become defensive. When questions arise, lean forward, ask clarifying questions, and keep your cool.

Avoid distracting mannerisms. Avoid any mannerisms that would distract your audience. The most common are clicking pens, shuffling papers or note cards, hands in pockets, ums and ahs, fidgety feet and fingers, swaying, and pacing. These nervous distractions should be avoided. Practicing the presentation will assist you in controlling nervous behaviors. Place your papers or pen down on the lectern. Keep both feet on the floor, and use your hands to make natural gestures or place them on the lectern in front of you.

Use humor. Presentations that are most enjoyable and are most remembered incorporate humor. Use humorous stories or analogies to keep the audience listening. Some people are better at making people laugh than others. If you are not a person who can naturally use humor, a few amusing remarks is all you should attempt. However, some speakers can maintain an audience's attention by finding humor in many of life's mundane situations.

Activities. If you are speaking for more than seven minutes, plan an activity so your audience will become an interactive part of your presentation. The activity can be a simple discussion question or a sampling of your product. Either way, involve the audience.

Practice

The sales presentation is important to your career. Take the time to practice. Practice in front of a mirror. Practice in front of other people who will be honest about the positive points of the presentation and areas to improve. It is also important that you videotape your presentation for your purview. At the very least, listen to an audiotape of the presentation. Do a dress rehearsal with the presentation aids you will use, and time the presentation in its entirety. Identify areas to improve and practice again. Practice will not only make you more effective, it will increase your confidence.

Personal Appearance

Now that you are prepared, practiced, and scheduled to present, dress the part. You should be the best dressed person in the room. However, if everyone will be in jeans, you would want to wear business casual. The majority of sales presenters should wear a well-fitted suit. Arrive early, check yourself in a mirror before you present, and appear confident. Being dressed like a professional boosts confidence levels.

Summary

In this chapter instruction was provided for creating a presentation to sell a product or service to potential customers. The sales presentation implements many of the skills addressed throughout this text. It incorporates research, powerful listening and delivery techniques, speaking that motivate others to action, and responses to impromptu questioning. The activity at the end of the chapter will be helpful if you are planning to present a sales presentation.

Preparing for the Sales Presentation

1. Define your product or service. _____
_____

2. List the advantages of your product and service to potential clients.

   _____
   _____
   _____
   _____
   _____
   _____
   _____

3. List any weaknesses about your product or service that you need to consider.

   _____
   _____
   _____
   _____

4. Write a brief history of your organization or business.

   _____
   _____
   _____
   _____
   _____

5. List target audience and specific advantages of your product or service as it relates to those potential clients.

   _____

   _____

   _____

   _____

   _____

   _____

   _____

6. List ten potential clients that you will contact. You need to research the top manager or person who makes the decisions to purchase the product or service that you are selling.

   _____

   _____

   _____

   _____

   _____

   _____

   _____

7. After you have made arrangements to present to a specific client, research that organization. Read the company or organization's Web sites. Search the Internet and newspapers for articles or advertisements about the company. Schedule a time to go to the company and walk around and talk to employees. You want to understand the culture and needs of the organization. Take notes, but at the very least you should know the:

   a. Mission and vision statements: _____

      _____

      _____

      _____

b. History of the organization: _____

_____

_____

_____

c. Current projects or priorities: _____

_____

_____

_____

d. Specific needs and goals with which your product or service
will meet: _____

_____

_____

_____

8. Situational questions.

Address: Room size:
Technology available:
Number of people who will attend: Time allotted for your
presentation:

9. Objections that may arise and ways to answer any objections.

_____

_____

_____

_____

_____

_____

_____

10. Goals or objectives of your presentation.

_____

_____

_____

_____

_____

_____

_____

_____

Presentation Outline Template

Introduction

    I. Attention Grabber: (Question, story, quote, humor, statistic, startling statement or action, current event.)

_____

_____

_____

_____

_____

    II. Introduction of presenters.

_____

_____

_____

_____

_____

    III. Brief history of your organization.

_____

_____

_____

_____

_____

    IV. Preview of the presentation.

_____

_____

_____

_____

_____

Body

I. Clearly explain your product or service.

_____

_____

_____

_____

_____

II. Explain the need of the organization.

_____

_____

_____

_____

_____

III. How your product or service will assist the organization in meeting their goals or needs.

_____

_____

_____

_____

_____

IV. Vividly explain how the organization will increase in productivity or sales if they buy your product or service. You may want to give an example of how a client has flourished by the use of the product or service.

_____

_____

_____

_____

_____

V. Give details about the costs. Explain costs in relationship to benefits and value as it relates to the competition.

_____

_____

_____

_____

_____

Conclusion

I.   Signal the conclusion.

_____

II. Summary of the need, satisfaction of the need, costs, and bottom line benefits.

_____

_____

_____

_____

_____

III. Powerful ending. Refer back to attention grabber, a memorable quote, a new dramatic story.

_____

_____

_____

_____

_____

IV. The close.

    1.   Encourage the audience to ask questions.
    2.   Ask if they would like you to write a contract.
        a.   If yes, then get a contract ready.
        b.   If concerns, negotiate and arrange for another meeting time.

References

ChangingMinds.org. (n. d.). *LACE.* Retrieved from http://changingminds. org/disciplines/sales/objection/objection_lace.htm

Cox, B. (n. d.). Believe in your product. Evan Carmichael. Retrieved from http://www.evancarmichael.com/Work-Life/3346/Believe-in-Your-Product.html

Hayden, C. J. (2007). *Get clients now!* 2nd ed. New York: AMACOM.

Parinello, A. (1999). *Selling to VITO: The very important top officer,* 2nd ed. Avon, MA: Adams Media.

Sjodin, T. L. *New sales speak: The 9 biggest sales presentation mistakes and how to avoid them,* 2nd ed. Hoboken, NJ: John Wiley & Sons, Inc.

Zini, A. (2009, July). Fast lane: Building a base. *Smart Business.* Retrieved from http://www.sbnonline.com/Local/Article/17809/79/0/Building_a_base.aspx?page=2

Chapter Eleven

Special Occasion Speeches

The objectives of this chapter are to:

- ✓ Identify various types of commemorative presentations.
- ✓ Understand how to organize toasts, roasts commemorative presentations, presentation speeches, and speeches of acceptance.
- ✓ Differentiate between types of keynote addresses.
- ✓ Compare symposium and panel presentations.
- ✓ Demonstrate emceeing, facilitating an event, and introducing a speaker.

Basic speech courses focus on students giving informative and persuasion speeches. However, in our personal lives, we are often called upon to present or we should step up and present for special occasions. If you are going to bring people together for any special event or ceremony, the person or persons bringing the group together should give a presentation. For instance, if a person hosts a shower, birthday party, retirement party, or graduation celebration, someone should give a presentation about why this person should be congratulated. If a group of people are giving any award, the person receiving the award should be publicly recognized for the achievement. Speakers called upon to give a presentation should be properly introduced. When an award is received, the recipient graciously explains his or her appreciation. The purpose of a special occasion speech is to praise, memorialize, or thank a person or group of people. There are also occasions when people come together and a person is called on to give a keynote address. This chapter explains the format for different types of tributary and keynote speeches.

Commendation Presentations

In many events, it is important to speak up and pay tribute to the guest of honor at a retirement, birthday, promotion, graduation, or anniversary celebration. This is a time of congratulations. One may pay tribute with a toast or roast, or one may simply stand before the group and briefly offer a heartfelt congratulation while telling of the notable qualities of the honoree(s). The presenter may want to tell a story about a noble accomplishment and then explain why this person is worthy of admiration.

Toasts

Toasts may be given anytime someone wants to speak up and wish another person love, happiness, congratulations, success, or friendship. Toasts are traditional at weddings but may be offered at just about any gathering such as a birthday party, anniversary celebration, retirement party, shower, Mother's Day, Father's Day, New Year's Eve, and Thanksgiving. If you are going to offer a toast, make sure that all glasses are full. Toasts do not require alcohol, but everyone needs to be holding a drink. Also, you may stand or sit and ask for everyone's attention, but do not bang on something or hit your glass with a utensil (Lininger, 2011).

After politely getting the attention of everyone at the table or in the room, hold up your glass at about waist level and offer a short, memorable, and prepared presentation. This should be about the person being honored, not the person offering the toast. Appropriate use of humor is fine, but keep the toast brief, and it should offer a tribute and goodwill to the person being honored by your toast. Then raise your glass to about eye level and conclude with a statement such as "To your future success" or "To your long and happy lives, together."

Toasts should be answered with a "thank you" and sip of beverage. Other, very brief spontaneous toasts may follow, so do not guzzle after a toast is offered. You may want to write a few lines of sentiment and memorize them. Paul Dickson (2008) wrote a book of one thousand five hundred toasts. One of his quotes is a parent toast at a wedding reception.

> It is written as follows:
> "When children find true love,
> parents find true joy."
> Here's to your joy and ours,
> from this day forward
> —*Parents' toast*

Roasts

Roasts are another type of a tribute. A roast should be planned, practiced, and humorous. When giving a roast, you do poke fun of the person being honored, but do not be offensive. You should really know the person you are roasting and the person's sense of humor. Some people are better at being laughed at than others. Get together with other people who know this person and make a list of amusing observations or habits this person has. From there, make some simple, short jokes. The jokes need to be appropriate to the occasion and the person being roasted. The jokes are good-natured but do not embarrass the person being roasted or anyone else. You may also use anecdotes that are true or exaggerated.

The roast should be brief. Start with a heartfelt tribute, go into a humorous body, and end with seriously expressing your admiration and respect for the honoree. You can tell stories and even exaggerate occurrences. There are probably things about the person that everyone already knows. For example, I had a student give a roast at a Toastmasters Club, and I was the honoree. She said, "You would be more likely to see an Amish family in a red sports car than to see Dr. Ruth without a coffee mug." The roast should be fun but still commemorate the honoree. At the end, the recipient of the roast should be given an opportunity to respond (Toastmasters International, 2011).

Speeches of Presentation

When a person is being given an award, the award needs to be publically presented with a speech of presentation. Companies, schools, community groups, competitions, and other organizations present awards. These are brief presentations where you tell why the speaker is receiving the award. Mention the losers, not by name, but announce how many people were nominated and why this person rose above the rest. This presentation mentions the hard work, dedication, sacrifices, and efforts of the recipient. Also, explain the significance of the award. The award should be displayed for everyone to see. When presenting the award, turn slightly to face the audience, give the person the award with your left hand, and shake the recipient's right hand. Then give the recipient a few minutes to give an acceptance speech (Toastmasters International, 2011).

Acceptance Speeches

Speeches accepting awards are very brief and serve to humbly thank the organization giving the award. Mention the organization and the award by name. Then, comment on this organization's contribution to you, the community, and/or your field of study. Tell the audience your emotions in receiving the award and what it means to you now and in the future. Also, acknowledge people who have helped you achieve your successes. Do not downplay the award or yourself, nor do you want to sound arrogant. To accept the award, turn slightly toward the audience, shake the presenter's right hand, and accept the award with your left hand.

Eulogies

A eulogy is a speech to pay tribute to a deceased friend or family member. These speeches should be a celebration of the person's life while giving comfort to those present. Eulogies need not be gloomy but should praise accomplishments and legacies. As with any speech, begin with an attention grabber. Then tell accomplishments and stories that capture the personality of the person being honored. Explain the person's qualities and attributes that made him or her unique and admired. Explain what you will miss the most and what you will remember and treasure from the experience of knowing this person.

Keynote or Guest Speaker

A keynote address is not limited to a professional speaker who comes to a company or convention to motivate the audience. These are indeed keynote addresses, but keynote addresses can also be given by a leader in the organization, at a commencement ceremony or as an after-dinner speech. What do these have in common, they are motivational in nature.

Organizational or Convention Keynote Addresses

To prepare for the keynote address, you should refer to the Motivational Speech chapter in this book to explain models of motivational speaking. If you are the keynote speaker for a business or organization, know the purpose, goal, and mission of the company. Ask about the organization's plan and what type of change they want to encourage. Also, understand the mission statement of the organization and those who work there. If you are speaking at a convention or any other event, discover the theme of the event and emphasize the theme and goals throughout. You may also research recent accomplishments within the organization and highlight these while motivating them to face challenges. Use what you know in your attention grabber and throughout the presentation.

To organize any keynote address, have a definite introduction, body, and conclusion. Start with a powerful title, attention grabber, and a preview. Have three points that are witty and memorable. Then explain how following your points will make our lives better. End with something intriguing and inspiring, such as a story. In his article, "11 Presentation Lessons You Can Still Learn from Steve Jobs," Carmine Gallo (2012) discussed the importance of being passionate about your topic, providing a great story with a problem, and then selling the audience on the benefits of what you have to offer. Keynote addresses bring benefits to the listener, motivating an audience to make their lives and the company better.

Commencement Addresses

Commencement addresses are designed to motivate graduates at a graduation ceremony. You are there because you have had successes. However, the speech is not about the speaker. It is a speech to congratulate and inspire the graduates. Commencement speeches should only be ten minutes or less. Congratulate the graduates, offer words of wisdom, use unique phrases that they will remember, and let them go celebrate their day. In a commencement speech, a few words that will remain forever in their minds are better than a long presentation about your accomplishments.

After-Dinner Speeches

Although there are after-dinner speeches in speech contests that are not given after a meal, a professional after-dinner speech is given after an audience has dined. As you can imagine, after a dinner, an audience will be drowsy and not in the mood for something that is overly serious. After-dinner speeches should be as entertaining as possible while being about an important topic. While coming up with an entertaining speech, center the purpose of the speech around the purpose of the event. This will assist you in identifying with the audience.

As with any special occasion speech, it should be brief (seven to fifteen minutes). It is not a stand-up routine, but it is a time to make a point while using funny stories, anecdotes, jokes, irony, puns, wit, and/or hyperbole. You can be funny without being offensive. In the end, pick an appropriate topic for the occasion and entertain the audience with content that will make them laugh out loud.

Symposium and Panel Presentations

Speakers who go to conventions to address audience in organizations or companies will present symposium or panel presentations. If an inept speaker presenting publically for his or her organization sends a poor message, it reflects poorly on the organization. As a speech professor and consultant, I have listened to more than one thousand speeches per year for more than a decade. Nonetheless, it is still startling to listen to speakers at conventions and professional events come ill prepared. I have heard eighteen-year-old students outperform speakers with doctorate degrees. If you are giving a presentation, prepare, practice, and impress!

Although symposiums and panels are often used synonymously, they are different. At conferences, symposiums and panel presentations are meant to be concise presentations of ten to thirty minutes. The speaker submits a brief abstract or a paper in the form of an article.

Panel requests in a conference are usually a request for a symposium presentation. In other words, each member of a symposium speaks about a topic on which he or she is an expert. Panelists express their views and respond to other panelists. Panels are conversations in front of the audience, whereas symposiums are individual speakers presenting a topic within his or her area of expertise.

When speaking at a conference, be prepared to engage your audience. These informative speeches need not be boring. Start with an attention grabber such as a story, quote, or statistic. Discuss your passion for and expertise in the subject area, and then preview your points. Next, highlight each point clearly while giving examples. Conclude your presentation with a signal, summary, and an emphasis on why this is important to the audience.

Practice so you do not need to read your presentation. It is important that you deliver your presentation using a conversational, energetic, and professional delivery style. Read the chapter in this book on immediacy behaviors. Connect with your audience by using exemplary eye contact, vocal variety, and a personable manner of speaking. If at all possible, engage your audience. You can ask questions or ask them to share an experience with a person sitting next to them. Interactive presentations are more enjoyable and much more memorable.

Go easy with the visual aids. If you are going to use a PowerPoint presentation, use more pictures, graphs, and video clips than words. You can have a slide with a single point and a picture that assists the audience in visualizing what you are talking about. A picture is worth a thousand words, and images are more meaningful and memorable. There is a TED Talk called "Talk nerdy to me" by Melissa Marshall; that is a wonderful example of how to present difficult information in an enjoyable, remarkable way.

Emcee or Facilitate Events

Emcees oversee special events, while focusing the audience's attention on the special guests or performers. The emcee should know everything they can about the event. It is important to meet each of the presenters or performers. Do not try to make introductions impromptu. Find out about the person's expertise. It is important to be enthusiastic, but do not make jokes or give a presentation (King, n.d.). The emcee is not the focus.

When introducing a speaker, do not read a resume. The *speech of introduction* should be one to two minutes, highlighting the person's expertise in the subject area on which he or she will be presenting. Discuss your introduction with the presenter or performer. Ask about name pronunciations. Write the introduction down and stay focused.

Be sure to practice your presentations and have everything in order well in advance. Do a soundcheck if you are using a microphone. In a kind way, get everyone's attention and welcome the audience. Very briefly introduce yourself and recognize anyone who helped with the planning or financing of the event. Be sure to use immediacy behaviors in your delivery.

The meeting facilitator or emcee stays out of sight between performances or presentations but near the stage so he or she can get to the lectern to shake the hand of the speaker leaving. You may want to make an interesting or humorous statement as a segue to the next speaker introduction. However, be very brief and do not say anything that would embarrass anyone. After your introduction, wait at the lectern to welcome the next presenter.

The emcee or facilitator is also responsible for keeping everything within a time frame. Let the speakers know of a signal when their time is almost up. If the speaker is going over time, walk onto the stage as a final signal. Keep all your comments brief and succinct. Finish the event with a planned final few words and thank everyone for being in attendance.

Summary

There are many opportunities to give presentations. It is important to give a well-prepared speech for special occasions or when presenting for a business or organization. Commemorative speeches pay tribute to others and should be given when celebrating the accomplishments or the life of friends and family. When you present a keynote address at an event or you are the facilitator of the occasion, make your presentations meaningful and memorable. Engage your audience in an experience that will enhance their lives.

Special Occasion Speech

You will be assigned a special occasion speech. Prepare the speech as instructed in the text. Each speech will have an introduction, body, and conclusion.

References

Academy of Motion Picture Arts and Sciences. (1998) *Academy Awards Acceptance Speech*. Retrieved from http://aaspeechesdb.oscars.org/link/070-24/

Dickson, P. (2008) *Toasts*. New York: Crown Publishers.

Gallo, C. (2012) "11 Presentation Lessons You Can Still Learn from Steve Jobs." *Forbes*. Retrieved from http://www.forbes.com/sites/carminegallo/2012/10/04/11-presentation-lessons-you-can-still-learn-from-steve-jobs/2/

King, C. (n.d.) "How to be an effective emcee." *Powerful Presentations*. Retrieved from http://www.creativekeys.net/powerfulpresentations/article1046.html

Lininger, M. (2011) "Toasting." *Etiquette Scholar*. Retrieved from http://www.etiquettescholar.com/dining_etiquette/toasts_and_toasting.html

Lutes, A. (2014) "The 13 Best Commencement Speeches of All Time Ever (Recently) So Far." *Nerdist*. Retrieved from http://www.nerdist.com/2014/05/the-13-best-commencement-speeches-of-all-time-ever-recently-so-far/

Toastmasters International. (2011) *Special Occasion Speeches*. Mission Viejo, CA: Toastmasters International.

Index